P9-BJA-475

Full of Hope and Promise

THE CANADAS IN 1841

Full
of Hope
and
Promise

ERIC ROSS

McGill-Queen's University Press
Montreal & Kingston • London • Buffalo

Legal deposit fourth quarter 1991
Bibliothèque nationale du Québec

Printed in Canada on acid-free paper

Publication of this book has been assisted by a grant
from the Marjorie Young Bell Fund, Mount Allison University,
and by the Canada Council through its Block Grant program.

Canadian Cataloguing in Publication Data

Ross, Eric, 1929–
Full of hope and promise : the Canadas in 1841
Includes bibliographical references.
ISBN 0-7735-0855-4
1. Québec (Quebec)—History—Fiction
2. Canada—History—1791–1841—Fiction. I. Title.
PS8585.0836F84 1991 C813'.54 C91-090221-6
PR9199.3.R68F84 1991

75087

Design and Production: Instructional Communications Centre,
McGill University.
The typeface used in the text is ITC Galliard®.

For
Clara Maisie Wells Ross

Contents

Preface

Ian Alexander Bell Robertson, the imaginary writer of this book, was invented by the author to describe the Canadas in 1841 in order to overcome a number of technical difficulties as well as to provide a means by which remarks of contemporary observers and material from newspapers might be easily integrated into the text. The five chapters forming the body of the work are edited versions of those left by Robertson at the time of his death in 1851. A number of stylistic changes – such as the shortening of sentences and reducing the number of commas so beloved by the author – were deemed necessary to make the work more accessible to the modern reader. The illustrations, their captions, and a number of footnotes have been added by the editor. So, too, have the many "boxes" that elaborate on matters referred to by Robertson in the text. The introduction, final chapter, and the afterword are also by the editor. Biographical information about Robertson has been imagined as follows.

Born in Lady Stair's Close, Edinburgh, in 1771, of prosperous parents, Robertson was educated privately at home before being sent to the [Royal] High School, where he displayed a lively mind, although he was perhaps better remembered for his successes in the yards than in the classroom. Between 1786 and 1790 he attended lectures in Edinburgh University, but left without taking a degree. While there, he was a founding member of "The Club," a group that met to discuss the social and political questions of the day. Among its members were Thomas Douglas, later Lord Selkirk, and Walter Scott, the novelist. All three were to remain lifelong friends.

After he left the university, Robertson read law with a view to becoming an advocate. He became increasingly drawn to the pen, however, and wrote a number of short pieces for the *Edinburgh Review*. These articles received some public favour and he was encouraged to attempt several novels, none of which found wide acceptance.

In his middle years, Robertson fell increasingly under the influence of Lord Selkirk and came to share his concern for the poor of the Scottish Highlands. Like Selkirk, he reached the conclusion that emigration would greatly assist in overcoming the region's economic difficulties. In 1811, when Selkirk was given his large land grant for a colony in Red River, Robertson resolved to offer his support by writing a description of the whole Northwest, as it was at that time, with a view to providing the intending settler with an intimate knowledge of the country. His manuscript was completed late in 1811. It was intended to be published under the title *Some Observations on the State of the Canadian Northwest in 1811*, but for reasons unknown today it was apparently set aside and eventually lost. Fortunately, in 1963, during the demolition of several old houses in George Square, it was discovered among a number of other writings in an attic and in 1970 was published for the first time.* In the same attic were several fragments of another manuscript, which have been assembled by the editor for publication here. It is almost certain they were prepared during Robertson's stay in Quebec, Lower Canada, from the spring of 1840 to the early summer of 1842. It would seem that Robertson was preparing a study of Upper and Lower Canada in 1841 either as a guide for the intending immigrant or, as is more likely, as a record of the colonies when they united and embarked on a promising future together. In any case, the work is restricted to 1841. Robertson barely mentions the Rebellions of 1837–38 and other events leading up to the union and it would seem that he had little interest in politics – unless, of course, there is a missing chapter. Fortunately, these matters have been well covered by later writers on this period. The strength of Robertson's work is that he provides a detailed backdrop of every day life against which these events took place. Thus his writing is of considerable interest today not only to those with a special interest in fields such as historical geography, social geography, sociology, economics, political science, and Canadian literature, but to the general reader as well.

---

* Eric Ross, *Beyond the River and the Bay: Some Observations on the State of the Canadian Northwest in 1811 with a View to Providing the Intending Settler with an Intimate Knowledge of that Country* (Toronto 1970, 1973)

Most of the writing was probably done in the well-stocked library of Robertson's merchant son in the St Louis quarter of Quebec. The son was justly proud of his fine collection of travel books, emigrant guides, and government reports. The elder Robertson was an inveterate newspaper reader and spent a great deal of time in the reading room of the Exchange, where both Canadian and British papers were to be found. During the summer of 1841 he undertook an extensive tour of the Canadas. Whether on a steamer or in a hotel or tavern, he seems to have passed many a pleasant hour going through the local papers, making notes and gathering information. There is also evidence to suggest that Robertson gleaned material from the libraries of several institutions in Canada, as well as from the Advocate's Library and the Signet Library in Edinburgh, after he returned to Scotland.

The style of writing, illustrations, and cartography are all designed to evoke a feeling of the period. All of the newspapers and many of the books in the bibliography would have been accessible to Robertson. Exceptions are a number of works by more recent writers, which have been used sparingly. Modern geographical jargon and terminology have been studiously avoided.

The author wishes to acknowledge a generous grant from the Canada Council in support of his work. He would also like to thank the staff of the National Archives of Canada, National Library of Canada, British Library, National Library of Scotland, University of Edinburgh Library, McGill Redpath Library, McCord Museum, Toronto Public Library, Library of the Royal Commonwealth Society (London), Queen's University Archives, Bishop's University Library, Dalhousie University Library, Library of the Quebec Literary and Historical Society, National Archives of Quebec, Mount Allison Ralph Pickard Bell Library, and the Carleton University Library.

Introduction

On 10 February 1841 Upper and Lower Canada were united to form the Province of Canada. For those who favoured the union the date was a happy choice, since it also marked the first anniversary of the union in marriage of Queen Victoria and her beloved Prince Albert. For the many French Canadians who were opposed to the union the date must have seemed more ominous, since 10 February was also the date when Canada had been officially handed over to the British in 1764. French Canadians had survived eight decades of British rule, but could they now survive assimilation in a united Canada with an English-speaking majority? To English Canadians, assimilation seemed as natural and as desirable a solution to ethnic diversity as it did to their American cousins to the south. And what better way to accomplish this worthy objective than to create a union in which English-speakers, reinforced by a steady stream of immigrants from Great Britain, would form an ever increasing majority? To French Canadians, who had struggled so long and so hard to retain a toehold for their language and religion in North America, union was an abomination. Indeed, in 1841, many of their leaders were still smarting from an unsuccessful earlier attempt to rush a union bill through the British Parliament during the summer of 1822. That episode was remembered as a furtive attempt by the English to dominate the French in a legislature where English-speaking members would outnumber the French. The English had wanted control of the assembly of a united Canada in order to further economic development. The French wanted to retain control of the assembly of Lower Canada to protect their distinctive heritage.

Ever since the natural unity of the St Lawrence River and the Great Lakes had been disrupted by the division of Canada into the provinces of Upper Canada and Lower Canada in 1791, the centrifugal forces that had led to the division in the first place struggled against the centripetal forces that were drawing it back together. Centrifugal forces were mostly ethnic: English-speaking Upper Canada was separated from predominantly French-speaking Lower Canada, in contrast, centripetal forces were largely economic: the need to improve navigation and trade along the St Lawrence and Great Lakes. The union of 1841 represented a temporary triumph of centripetal forces. An important contribution to their triumph was a £1.5 million loan guarantee from the British Treasury towards the completion of the St Lawrence canals on condition that the union take place.

In the early days when furs dominated trade with the interior, the rapids on the St Lawrence and Ottawa rivers were of little consequence since cargoes were carried in light canoes that could easily be portaged. Large crews were required, but because the furs and the goods exchanged for them had a high unit value, they could bear the high cost of transport. Montreal, as the centre of the fur trade, drew much of its wealth from the interior. As recently as the 1790s, furs had made up half the value of all exports from the St Lawrence. By 1810, however, they had dropped to only 10 per cent. By the time the Montreal-based North West Company merged with the Hudson's Bay Company in 1821, furs were even less significant. The relative decline in the importance of furs was brought about by the rapid settlement of Upper Canada during the late eighteenth and early nineteenth centuries. Montreal, which had controlled the fur trade, now focused increasingly on exporting Upper Canadian potash, wheat, flour, pickled pork, and wood to Great Britain. Manufactured goods and immigrants from the old country made up the return haul. Furs had been shipped mostly by way of Lake Superior and the Ottawa River, whereas the new trade was focused largely on the upper St Lawrence–Lake Ontario route. These bulky commodities required larger and sturdier vessels than was generally the case with the fur trade. At first, bateaux were used. Although small, they were not portaged but rather wrestled up the rapids, with one man remaining in the bateau while three or more others tugged on a line from on shore or while wading in the frigid river. To facilitate the upward journey, small locks were constructed at some of the rapids. On the downward journey, the bateaux shot the rapids. As traffic increased, much larger, flat-bottomed Durham boats were introduced and the need for greater improvements in navigation on the St Lawrence became more compelling. Neither the bateaux nor the Durham boats could be used on the Great Lakes. This inconvenience inspired

Montreal merchants to dream of wide canals with large locks, which would allow ships from Lake Ontario to make the trip to Montreal without the transshipment of goods. Their city would then control the trade of Upper Canada and would become the grand emporium for the trade of the whole interior of North America. However, there was one catch: since 1825 the Americans had been diverting much of Montreal's "natural" trade to New York by way of the "artificial" Erie Canal. The canal linked Lake Erie at Buffalo with the Hudson River. Although the Erie Canal was still quite narrow in 1841, it had the advantage of a longer ice-free season than the St Lawrence. Not only was it handling much of the American trade between the Great Lakes and the eastern seaboard, but it was also beginning to challenge Montreal's hegemony over the Upper Canada trade. The rapidly growing network of railroads in the United States posed another threat to the supremacy of the St Lawrence.

Montreal's future could best be assured in a united province working towards improvements in navigation and trade. At least, that was the view of the mostly English-speaking mercantile class. Most upper Canadian farmers and merchants with products for export would have agreed, but the farmers of Lower Canada could see little advantage to themselves in supporting the expensive works required. Nor could the French-speaking middle class of Lower Canada, based as it was largely on land and agriculture. Even so, there were exceptions. A number of French Canadians did abandon the small, intimate, inward-looking domain of their own people to join the largely British and American mercantile community with its strong links to the outside world. From their establishments near the wharves at Montreal the merchants could look out and see the chunky little steamers belching black smoke as they towed tall, ocean-going sailing ships into the crowded harbour. Similar scenes could be seen at Quebec. The ships with the pungent odour – they could be detected more than a mile away – were crowded with immigrants from Great Britain. The smaller vessels were likely from the "lower provinces" of New Brunswick and Nova Scotia, while others might be from the United States, the West Indies, and even from distant places like New South Wales and Van Diemen's Land.

When the British government brought about the union of the Canadas in 1841, the merchants were delighted. In effecting a union, the government was acting on one of the recommendations made by Lord Durham following his mission to Canada in the aftermath of the 1837 Rebellions. To carry out the new policy, a new type of governor general was sent to Canada in the autumn of 1839. Charles Poulett Thomson had more in common with the commercially oriented Durham than with his other predecessors: he was neither a military man nor a member of the landed gentry, but the son of a London merchant. Before coming to Canada Poulett Thomson had spent two prolonged stints in a branch of his father's firm in St Petersburg; he had also been a member of parliament and a president of the Board of Trade. With this background he was well equipped to carry out the delicate task of effecting a union and establishing a new constitution.

Under the young and energetic governor general – Poulett Thomson was still only thirty-nine when appointed – economic progress overrode most other considerations. He worked quickly: he knew that before economic progress was possible union was necessary. And before union was feasible the many centrifugal forces that stood in its way had to be eliminated or, at least, tightly reined in. With great skill, tact, and hard work, he managed to redirect these forces and succeeded in getting agreement for a new constitution through the colonial parliaments and ratified by the House of Commons. He also carried a measure for local government (which resulted in the merchants gaining more power in the cities) and initiated improvements in immigration, education, and public works. It was a remarkable accomplishment and gained Poulett Thomson a peerage: on 19 August 1840 he was raised to Baron Sydenham of Sydenham in Kent and Toronto.

Durham had recommended responsible government along with union. This was only partly carried out under Lord Sydenham. The Executive Council would now consist of department heads who held seats in the Assembly, but Sydenham acted as his own prime minister. This arrangement turned out to be a transitional phase to true responsible government a few years later. However, in 1841 it was enough to encourage moderate reformers in both Upper and Lower Canada to support the union. At the same time, the governor's retention of power partly assuaged the fears of the more conservative elements, especially those who had long regarded themselves as the natural rulers, of finding themselves subjected to the "excesses of democracy." The Rebellions of 1837 and 1838 had left a legacy of bitter distrust between English and French, between those who wished to reform government by giving more power to the people and those who opposed change, and between those who sought independence or union with the United States and those who wished to remain loyal to the crown. With good judgment, prudence, and an ability to speak French, Sydenham succeeded in winning over a large number with conflicting aspirations, but he could not hope for complete success. At both extremes there were men – among them fanatics – who would not be budged towards the centre.

Kingston was chosen as the capital of the new province. The French-Canadian member would now be forced to leave his familiar cocoon to take up residence during the session in the "free air" of an English city. Here, he would encounter "a more enterprising, progressive and commercial spirit." Undoubtedly this would inspire him to vote in the legislature for "progress" and to emulate this spirit when he returned to his home riding after the session.

Kingston was the smallest of the possible choices for the capital. The wild little lumber centre of Bytown had never been a realistic candidate. The fact that Kingston won out over the other possibilities was indicative of the weakness of the union. In Canada, there was no London or Paris to provide a unifying focus. There was only compromise. Kingston alone seemed satisfied with the choice.

In Quebec there was great unhappiness as the books of the legislative library – many dating far back into the French period – were crammed into barrels for shipment "into the wilderness." Always insecure, Toronto missed no opportunity to heap scorn on the "new metropolis." Even when Lord Sydenham was critically injured in a fall from his horse, a Toronto newspaper could not resist using the occasion to criticize the rocky soil in the capital. Montrealers seemed more temperate. Possibly few people thought their city would become the capital, anyway, so there was little feeling of loss or resentment.

The union of the Canadas on 10 February 1841 was barely noticed in Great Britain. There was far more excitement about the baptism, on the same day, of the Queen's first child, Victoria, the Princess Royal and heir to the throne. Before the year was out the little princess dropped to second in line with the birth of Edward, the future Prince of Wales and Edward VII. An astrologer might have noted that 10 February had proved to be a propitious date for the fruitful union of Victoria and Albert. Would it also prove to be equally auspicious for the Canadas? By the end of 1841 there was reason for optimism.

Full of Hope and Promise

"But Canada has held, and always will retain, a foremost place in
my remembrance. Few Englishmen are prepared to find it
what it is. Advancing quietly; old differences settling down, and
being fast forgotten; public feeling and private enterprise
alike in a sound and wholesome state; nothing of flush or fever in its
system, but health and vigour throbbing in its steady pulse:
it is full of hope and promise."

– Charles Dickens, American Notes, 1842 –

Chapter I

Two
Peoples,
One
Country

Ian Alexander Bell Robertson liked Quebec. In a strange way it
reminded him of Edinburgh. The view of the citadel from the
Plains of Abraham "put him in mind," as he would say, of the view
towards Edinburgh Castle from across The Meadows. The squalid
streets of Lower Town evoked memories of the congested court-
yards and closes of Edinburgh's mediaeval High Street, and the
scene looking down on the St Lawrence from the new Durham Terrace reminded him of the view looking north to the Forth from
the castle esplanade. There was also a large measure of *déjà vu* in
many of his observations. In his younger years he had seen the
Edinburgh gentry abandon their cramped homes in the Old Town
for more spacious quarters in the New Town. Houses that had
once been occupied by noblemen were now lived in by tradesmen –
or worse. And now, in 1841, the same process was taking place in
Quebec. The lower Town was all but abandoned by the merchants,
and even those in the Upper Town were beginning to move out
to extensive estates on the Plains of Abraham. In his youth in
Edinburgh, members of differing social ranks often lived on the
same "stair" in the tall tenements of the Old Town where they
knew one another. With the building of the New Town, there was
a sorting out of various classes and occupations, and they became
strangers one to another. The same thing was now happening
in Quebec, and in other Canadian cities as well.

Robertson toured the Canadas during the summer of 1841 –
partly for pleasure and partly to gather material for his book. Although overwhelmed by the sublime scenery, he felt that the trip
had been somewhat redundant since, as he was wont to point out
with some frequency, one could find perfectly good examples of
every type of person living in the Canadas within a ten-minute

Quebec
by W.H. Bartlett.
In Willis, **Canadian Scenery,**
vol. 1, facing p. 49

walk from his son's residence in the St Louis quarter of the Upper Town. Indeed, it was here in the area in and around the Upper Town Market where he took his daily constitutional – just as he had in Edinburgh's Lawn Market – that he made many of his keenest observations about everyday life in the Canadas. Five years before coming to Quebec, Robertson had been to Sydney, New South Wales, to visit his other son, David, who was there as a member of the governor's suite. He had travelled out by way of Cape Town and returned via Calcutta. It was a great adventure for a man of sixty-five and accounts for his comparison of Quebec with those other colonial port capitals.

Robertson's Quebec son, Angus, was the Canadian partner in a Clydeside lumber firm. He had emigrated to Canada in his late twenties and was married to the daughter of a distinguished French-Canadian family. Through her, the elder Robertson was able to gain access to the largely closed society of French Canada. As a Scot, there was an unconscious tendency to identify with the French *vis-à-vis* the English. Yet in his writing there is an ambivalence in his view of the English. As a member of Edinburgh "society" he was part of the most Anglicized community in Scotland and, when convenient, he identified himself with the English. On other occasions, he is not above playing the Scot, poking fun at the English and their ways with more than a bit of irony. Like the upper-class Edinburgh Scot he was, he did not need a Tocqueville to remind him that members of the French-Canadian elite were likely to take on English ways first. When he speaks of the desirability of the French members of the new United Parliament learning English ways when they go up to Kingston, he is obviously remembering how effectively many a Scottish member had been assimilated at Westminister. In Canada, Robertson witnessed the "emigrant" becoming an "immigrant" and was not always edified by the result. Indeed, he could be quite harsh in discussing the way new settlers took on North American manners and buried their past – like many a Scot "going to the south" and aping the effete manners of the English. At the same time, Robertson was both fascinated and shocked by the levelling influences at work in the Canadas – a theme that is woven in throughout *Full of Hope and Promise*.

*E*nglish and French began life together in Canada in the damaged city of Quebec during the uneasy winter of 1759–60. A high degree of cooperation was necessary between Britain's new subjects (as the French were known) and her old subjects if both were to survive until spring in the newest – and coldest – city in the empire, and it was here that the pragmatic regimen unfolded that would govern their fretful relationship for decades to come. Its Frenchness has allowed Quebec to retain a flavour of its own, although by now it has evolved into a typical British colonial seaport capital. Among its residents are men and women who have lived previously in other remote parts of the empire and who now see in Quebec much that is familiar, whether they have come from Sydney in New South Wales, Cape Town in southern Africa, Kingston in Jamaica, or Calcutta in India: a fine harbour guarded by a citadel; a scarlet-coated parade square echoing to barked orders, snapping heels, and a military band; a governor's residence – access to which is *de rigeur* for social success; public buildings of solid Georgian design, imposed on an alien landscape by a presumptuous people who have come to stay; an Anglican cathedral with its broad royal pew and icons more of England than of God; a race track, a custom house, an assembly, a court house, and a jail.

The British preference is for order and symmetry, for parks and broad streets punctuated with open squares, but on occasion this has not been possible because of difficult terrain or previous settlement. Nowhere is this more evident than at Quebec, where the stunning site and inherited settlement have negated the rule of harmony and order.

The French chose a fine location for their principal settlement in America: a point 350 miles from the sea where the St Lawrence is pinched to a width of less than a mile by the Appalachians to the south and the mountains of the Canadian Shield to the north. From the river, the site seemed like a huge rock rising sharply from the water's edge, though in fact it is the prow of a long rocky ridge jutting into the stream. Along its base and between it and the St Charles River, which joins the main river just below the rock, stretched a narrow terrace on which Champlain founded the city in 1608. He had foreseen how the rock would protect his settlement from the cruel northwest winds, and he was also aware that a hundred ships might ride at anchor in the deep basin nearby. Land was scarce along the tiny terrace and soon a pattern of narrow, congested streets emerged in what came to be known as the Lower Town. From the Lower Town a narrow, winding road climbed up onto the irregular surface forming the cap of the rock. Here the French built their Upper Town, with its sprinkling of large religious and governmental buildings scattered on spacious, irregularly shaped lots. Streets filled in the gaps among them. Cape Diamond, the highest part of the rock – commanding both the Lower Town and the river – was set aside for the citadel. Except where the steepness of the rock's face made it unnecessary, the Upper Town was surrounded by a defensive wall.

After the conquest of 1759, the British gradually made Quebec their own: their governor moved into the old French governors' Palace of St Louis; their cathedral – an adapted and abridged model of London's St Martin's-in-the-Fields – replaced the burned Recollet church; their soldiers converted the Jesuit College – in its day said to be the largest building in North America – into a barracks; and so it went until, by 1841, the Upper Town has become predominantly English, although many French still hold on in order to be near their cathedral, hospital, convent, and seminary. However, they are becoming increasingly concentrated on the flats along the St Charles in the fast-growing suburb of St Roch. Others remain in the Lower Town, although they are now coming under greater pressure from the English poor and from the destitute Irish who are arriving each year in ever larger numbers. Most of the senior officers of the provincial government and people of the highest rank have chosen to live in the elevated part of the Upper Town, in and about St Louis Street. St Louis is one of the two principal streets of the Upper Town; the other is St Johns. Each penetrates the wall through a gate of the same name and each leads to a new suburb, just beyond the walls, also bearing its name. Like St Roch, both the St Johns and the St Louis suburb follow the well-ordered grid common to North American settlement. The Lower Town, with its back to the rock, has little chance for expansion except by squeezing towards St Roch or by pushing out into the River – and this it has done in recent years as some of the adjoining tidal flats have been reclaimed.

Upper Town Market, Quebec, showing the French cathedral, by J.P. Cockburn. Watercolour, pen and ink drawing. National Archives of Canada (NAC)

In Quebec can be found most of the elements that constitute the population of both Canadas: French Canadian, English, Scots, Irish, Indian, and a handful of others. Nowhere can they be better observed than in the Upper Town's Place d'Armes – unless it is in the market nearby. In this neighbourhood live the governor, the Anglican and Roman Catholic bishops, and most of the senior military and civilian officials. To their discomfort, the open spaces of the market and the square make it nearly impossible for them to call on one another without being seen – geography has precluded many secrets in Quebec. The market is visited regularly by all orders of society. In a variety of dress betraying their class and origin, they can be observed scrambling among the sleighs and steaming horse-buns of winter or among the carts and flies of summer as they search for the luxuries and necessities of life. Most of the vendors are French-Canadian peasants, or habitants, from the farms along the north shore of the St Lawrence or the Ile-d'Orléans. The women are usually dressed in homespun purples and reds, the men in coarse grey hooded capotes with brightly coloured sashes. Visitors from Great Britain are struck by their good manners and their universal kindness. Like the "natives" elsewhere, they are generally thought by the British to be "happy and contented" although on occasion they are stirred up by the few "trouble makers" among them.

Prices for the wood, hay, meat, wild pigeons, fruit, vegetables, flowers, and so on are not fixed and a great deal of clamouring in broken English and bad French is necessary before a sale is made. The fact that many people lose their teeth early in life does not make the bargaining any easier. In the half-light of a grey winter's dawn, the market takes on an air that is at once bizarre and ethereal. There is something dreamlike about the twitching, steaming flanks of the horses, their noses nearly pinned to the ground with icicles; the carcasses of cows and pigs frozen into grotesque shapes; solid milk being sold in cabbage bags; and everywhere men and women stamping their neat homemade boots and swinging their arms in great circles to keep out the cold. Even the frolicsome jingle of the sleigh bells and the dour cathedral's toll are curiously muffled as their sound drops into the snow.

As in Europe, the market faces the cathedral. It is on the edge of what is considered the mercantile part of the city – an area that extends down along St Johns and Palace streets into the lower elevations of the Upper Town. Here live the retail traders and artisans, numerous tavern keepers and merchants. The merchants have much in common with those in St Louis

Canadian Habitants by Mrs M.M. Chaplin. Watercolour, NAC

8

THE ANGLICAN CATHEDRAL

For English tastes, the Anglican cathedral provided a soothing counterpoint to the baroque splendour of its French counterpart. Its proportions were taken in great measure from St Martin's-in-the-Fields, London, but the state of materials and workmanship in Canada made a plain design necessary. The cathedral itself was only thirty-seven years old, but in its yard stood a noble elm reputed to date back three centuries and said to have witnessed the arrival of Cartier and to have sheltered Champlain when he pitched his tent under its branches at the founding of Quebec in 1608. On Sunday mornings a joyous eight-bell peal poured out its familiar cadences to greet the nostalgic young British soldier as he marched to his place during church parade. To his left, in the balcony, was the royal pew, emblazoned with the imperial arms. Like the other pews, and even the altar rail, it was made from oak sent out from England to this land of endless forests. Sitting in the front rows of the newly installed galleries on either side of the organ were a number of children. They were readily identified by their uniforms as orphans under the care of the congregation. In harmony with the spirit of the age, their presence enabled their benefactors to derive merit in the public eye for charity voluntarily and cheerfully performed; at the same time, the children were being taught to recognize the active benevolence in others without which their wants could not have been supplied. Thus, the rich, sitting erect in their Sunday best, profited from the poor just as the poor gained from the rich: each depended on the other. Like the bells and the pews, the clergymen were imported from England. James Silk Buckingham judged them to be inferior in talents to the general standard of the English church, with "rather more than the usual portion of formality."

The Anglican cathedral at Quebec. Metropolitan Toronto Reference Library, J. Ross Robertson Collection, 2006

INDIANS IN THE MARKET

Indians emerging into the crowded Upper Town market were often harried by pursuing dogs: something about them offended the sensibilities of the town-bred beasts. The Indians were from the village of Lorette and came in regularly to sell their baskets and game, or to beg. They paid little attention to the barking animals – even though some of the women carried small babies on their backs – except occasionally to hit out half-heartedly with a stick at any snarling snout that came too close. Dogs were a nuisance throughout the city in 1841, prompting authorities to place poison in the streets "for the benefit of animals running loose."

The Indians were descendants of the old Huron allies of the French. Over the years, there had been much intermixing with the French and, in physical appearance, they now seemed quite European. However, they preferred native dress and adhered to many of the old Indian ways. They were still outstanding hunters and fishermen and regularly hired themselves out as guides – even to gentlemen of the most respectable classes.

Street, yet they also mix easily with their trader and artisan neighbours. This friendliness probably has something to do with the fact that the merchants, like most of the retail traders and the more skilled artisans, are English.

As is common in many cities, the population of Quebec – 32,000 in 1841 – is sorting itself into various quarters according to class and national origin. Much of the Upper Town, however, is still fairly mixed and it is not at all uncommon for French and English to occupy neighbouring houses – although this proximity does not necessarily mean they are neighbours. Indeed, for the most part, English and French live in two separate worlds.

During the early days of British rule, language does not seem to have been much of a problem. Many of the higher ranks of the British population spoke French – they considered it a mark of accomplishment – although it was true that the lower orders placed little value on it. The upper classes did not hesitate to have their children educated in French and at least two of the governors general – Dorchester and Prescott – sent their daughters to the Ursuline Convent in Quebec. (It is conveniently situated just a few steps from the market in the direction of St Louis Street.) That the sisters were French and Roman Catholic was far less important than that they were drawn from the most respectable society of French Canada.

St John Street from the corner of Palace Street, showing English-language signs, by J.P. Cockburn. Detail, watercolour, pen and ink over pencil, Royal Ontario Museum

There were few English at first, but as their numbers were augmented – increasingly by members of the lower orders from Great Britain and from the other American colonies – ramparts were raised between the two peoples. Few English were drawn to farming in Lower Canada, since better land and more enticing climates could be found elsewhere. Most came to trade and located in the towns,

QUEBEC COURT HOUSE

Wealthy and powerful Quebeckers returning to their homes in the most respectable part of the Upper Town from the boisterous and often disorderly market usually passed the Court House, which stood on the upper edge of the Place d'Armes, like a sentinel, with its back to their homes and with its formal English facade gazing out over the less affluent parts of the city. At night its tin roof glowed softly in the moonlight above its harmonious Georgian bulk: for the wealthy, it was an assurance that order and peace will prevail; for the rest of the population, it was more intimidating. Drunkenness was common and was at the root of most crime. A few drinks too many at a market tavern after church on Sunday could end with a trip up the imposing double staircase and into one of the court rooms to face the full pomp and majesty of the law. High on the wall was an impressive painting of the British Arms; beneath it sat the judge, splendid in his robes and bands. Both languages were permitted in court. Depending on his religious persuasion, a witness might choose to kiss the silver Christ on the Bible and promise in French to tell the truth, or he might turn it over to the undecorated side and swear the same oath in English – to a bilingual God. One lawyer might be French, the other English. It was easier for each to think and to argue in his own tongue, although he might soon find himself speaking in his adversary's language as he warmed to his argument. If he became too heated, the court crier might intervene with a call for "silence," alternately using the French and English pronunciations.

leaving the countryside to the French. Before long, English became the accepted language of commerce and, by 1841, all commercial signs were in English – even those on shops and inns with French-Canadian proprietors in areas far removed from the English population. To the deaf traveller, Lower Canada must seem very English; to his blind companion, it is overwhelmingly French. In truth, it is about one-tenth English and nine-tenths French. Yet, in spite of these proportions, the English are becoming increasingly impatient with the French language. Lord Sydenham discovered this whenever he used his fluent French. It did not endear him to many of his fellow English-speaking Canadians.

The relative importance of the French and English languages has changed remarkably in the eight short decades since the Conquest. France has gone through the Revolution, the Napoleonic defeat, and is now suffering from population stagnation. By contrast, England is thriving and her people and language are spreading into every corner of the globe – the United States alone now has a population of 17 million. English is no longer merely the language of a small country at the edge of Europe. Almost overnight, it has become the tongue of many millions both at home and abroad as well as the language of international trade and of the seas. All of these changes are reflected in the relationships between English and French in Canada.

As each decade passes, the English in Canada are becoming more and more cavalier in their dealings with the French. This failing has not been overlooked by certain visitors from the old country. For instance, John M'Gregor noted in 1832 that the English not only "assumed an arrogant superiority over the French" but that they did so at a time when the French were far above them "in the scale of manners and acquirements which shed lustre over, and give a tone of well-bred gentility to, society." Lord Durham agreed when he suggested that "it is not anywhere a virtue of the English race to look with complacency on any manners, customs or laws which appear strange to them."

Even more recently – indeed, during the past year – James Silk Buckingham, the noted travel writer, made similar observations. The French have remained, he said "as much separated from the English up to the present time, as they were within the first ten years after the conquest." Buckingham places most of the blame on the English, who he feels have been guilty of not inviting the French to attend their societies, to learn their language, or to exchange their hospitalities – at least not on a sufficient scale to ensure any degree of amalgamation. The responsibility of making the social overtures has lain with the English. After all, the French, as the conquered people, wold have been unwilling to press themselves on the society of their new masters. They were little inclined to learn any language but their own and were filled with prejudices imbibed with their religion. Moreover, they were less wealthy than the English. Buckingham sees no similar excuses for a greater effort not having been made on the British side. As the more powerful, the more wealthy, and the more free from religious prejudices, he believes they should have done everything in their domain to make the yoke sit lightly on the necks of those who were obliged to wear it. It is his experience that the English mingle more easily with the French in Paris or with the Italians in Naples than they do with the French in Canada. Perhaps it should be pointed out that Buckingham's stay has been at a time when English-French relations are abnormally strained. In any case, the problem does not lie in the quality of the French spoken in Canada: several visitors have compared it favourably with that spoken in Paris, and the geologist Charles Lyell, who lived in France before his recent visit to Canada, believes that the French spoken in the provinces of the mother country is often less correct, and less easy to follow, than that of the Canadians. He liked the French Canadians as a people and was struck by their prepossessing manners, "much softer and more polite than those of their Anglo-Saxon fellow-countrymen, however superior the latter may be in energy and capability of advancement."

Implicit in the observations of many British visitors is the desirability of the assimilation of the French Canadian into the modern world. Indeed, for some, the Conquest is seen as a release from the shackles of the past, a chance to leave behind the backward and the outmoded, an opportunity to enter the future – which is English. Not unexpectedly, this view is not shared by that keenest of French observers, Alexis de Tocqueville, who came to Canada in 1831, before the rebellions and in a period when there was more mixing between the races, particularly among the better educated. He was startled to discover that some members of the "enlightened class" of French Canadians seemed "near to merging with the English" and that many of them were not animated to the extent he had expected "by the wish to keep the trace of their origin intact." Tocqueville places a high value on the preservation in Canada of "the race, language and custom of the French" and views with distaste any move towards the eventual amalgamation of the two peoples. The term "English" is used loosely by Tocqueville and others, and commonly includes the Welsh, Scots and Irish. The Scots and Irish cause Tocqueville the most concern: the Irish Catholics who might fuse with the French, and a small but important group of men, many of them Scots, who have already bridged the two races.

It is not difficult to spot the Irish in the Upper Town market. Some come to beg, some to buy, most appear desperately poor – often dressed only in rags, their bare legs gaining them the sardonic sobriquet *bas de soie* or silk-stocking. Because they are often Roman Catholic in religion and English in language, it is commonly held that they have been sent among the French Canadians to absorb them. (Louis-Joseph Papineau has gone even further and has suggested that the British injected the country with the "cholera-Irish" in order to eliminate the French-Canadian population.) The vessels bringing the Irish are among the worse of the immigrant ships; there is no mistaking them – the stench of packed humanity creeps ahead on the breeze to warn of their impending arrival. John Bigsby, a former medical officer at Quebec, described the vessels as little more than "itinerant pest-houses," without proper provisions and "fitted up almost slave-ship fashion by the agents of impoverished and unprincipled landlords." Only a small portion of the waves of Irish who survive the voyage and who wash up each year on the Canadian shore remain at Quebec; most manage somehow to trickle up country – often on charity or with government aid – and on into Upper Canada or the United States.

Scottish soldiers, and some newly arrived Scottish immigrants, are easily identified in the market square by the kilt. (Back in 1759–60, when Canadian ladies were not yet accustomed to seeing the bare legs of men in public, a bond was formed between Scot and

Irish immigrants (left) by J.P. Cockburn. Detail of a drawing. Royal Ontario Museum

Scottish soldier in the market place. Detail from **The Market Place, Quebec** *by W.H. Bartlett. In Willis,* **Canadian Scenery,** *vol. 2, facing p. 11*

French when the nuns at Quebec knitted long woollen stockings to shield bony Highland knees from the swirling updrafts of winter – and from sight.) Many of the earlier soldiers took their discharge in Canada and settled in and around Quebec. Most prospered and were later joined by relatives and others from the old country. Among these was John Neilson who, like a number of others over the years, married a French Canadian. He became the publisher of the bilingual *Quebec Gazette* and, as such, was one of the chief spokesmen for the small group linking the two peoples. Neilson was a member of the Reform party and, although a Protestant, managed to represent a largely French constituency in the House of Assembly of Lower Canada from 1818 to 1834. In 1834 he broke with the extreme reformers under Papineau and was defeated, but now, in 1841, he is back representing his old constituency in the new parliament of united Canada – although, like most French Canadians, he did not approve of the union. It is men like Neilson who made Tocqueville uneasy: true, they are accepted by the French Canadians and their interests are more French than English, but deep down they are "English in manners, ideas and language." "If ever they take the place of the upper classes and of the enlightened classes among the French Canadians," he wrote, "the nationality of the latter will be lost without reprieve. They will vegetate like the people of Lower Brittany in France." Fortunately for the continuance of French culture, religion has placed an obstacle in the way of mixed marriages, although it has not deterred couples like the Neilsons.

Mixed families are still quite exceptional in the Lower Canada of 1841 and are largely confined to the cities. Most French Canadians belong exclusively to what may be called *the* French-Canadian family or nation; they are descendants of the original French stock of fewer than 9000 souls, almost all of whom came from France at least a century and a half ago. This number is minuscule compared with the throngs of immigrants now pouring in from the British Isles, a number that in 1841 is eclipsed once again in a single year. The French migrants formed a much more homogeneous people than the so-called "English," whose origins can be traced back not only to England, Scotland, Ireland, Wales, Orkney, Jersey, the Isle of Man, and the United States, but even, on occasion, to Germany, Holland, or Switzerland. Unlike the French, who are virtually all Roman Catholic, the English follow a spectrum of faiths ranging from Catholicism to Unitarianism; there is even a handful of Jews among them. Few countries offer greater religious tolerance than Canada both in law and in practice. French Canadians worship as they always have, and it is the gathering each Sunday at the church door to exchange news of the week's happening that, more than anything else, has kept the community united. The English, of course, also go to church, but since they attend a variety of denominations the effect is to reinforce diversity rather than unity.

The original French settlers were drawn from widely scattered areas in their homeland. In Canada they took root, reaching 65,000 at the time of the Conquest and by 1841, over 600,000 – almost totally through natural increase. All personal ties with France have long since been broken; they belong only to Canada and think of themselves only as "Canadians." Terms such as "French" and "French Canadians" are left to the strangers who live among them and who have retained attachments elsewhere.

As recently as 1830 there lived near the market an old gentleman who had served under Wolfe in the Battle of the Plains of Abraham; in 1841 one can still see occasionally – picking among the market stalls – the stooped figure of one or other of the few remaining Canadians whose earliest memories are of a time when Quebec was still the capital of New France. Their lifetimes have witnessed the arrival of the first few hundred English and have seen their numbers swell to more than 500,000 in the two Canadas. Most of the increase has come with the surge of immigration during the past twenty-five years.

No French Canadian can look down from the Upper Town on the arriving hordes of immigrants below without a feeling of desolation: many of these loud, rude, uncouth strangers are destined for land he has regarded as his own – some of it within sight of where he is standing. Tocqueville was puzzled by the way the French Canadians had allowed themselves to become increasingly hemmed in by the English. When he asked one of them why his people had allowed themselves to be confined to their narrow fields when they could have found fertile, uncultivated land only twenty leagues from home, he was answered: "Why do you love your wife best, although your neighbour's has more beautiful eyes?" Few English feel a similar attachment for the lands on which they live or even for the plot they have laboriously cleared; if they see a better opportunity, they move on without hesitation – even if it means leaving behind friends or relations or, perhaps, going to another country. If there is one thing the English hold in common, it is a desire to improve themselves and their families in terms of the good things of this life.

In shops near the Upper Town market, and elsewhere in Canada, books on India, Australia, the West Indies, and Africa remind the English that Canada is but a small part of an ever expanding English-speaking world made up of the British Empire and the United States. So, too, do their newspapers with their columns of imperial and American news. If they are farmers, they can seek advice in the

THE MONTREAL MERCHANT

In both Quebec and Montreal, many of the merchants – most of whom were English speaking – lived in the central part of the city. To ensure that their interests would prevail in the parliament of the united Canadas, Sydenham lopped off the suburbs of both cities. It was, he said "a question between four English or four French Canadian members both now and hereafter." One of the two members elected for the Montreal City riding in 1841 was George Moffatt. He had run with Lord Sydenham's blessing in spite of His Excellency's belief that Moffatt was "the most pig headed, obstinate, ill tempered brute in the Canadas."

Moffatt is worth mentioning since he was typical of the Montreal businessmen of the 1840s. He came to Canada from England in 1801 under the sponsorship of William Nelson Ogilvy, a Montreal merchant who was involved in the fur trade. In 1811 Moffatt entered the trade on his own and set up a company that eventually became known as Gillespie, Moffatt, and Company. (Robert Gillespie was his London partner.) By 1821, the year of the merger of the North West Company and the Hudson's Bay Company, which was facilitated by Moffatt, the firm of Gillespie, Moffatt, and Company was one of the largest import-export houses of Montreal. It had diversified far beyond the fur trade and dealt in a wide variety of imported goods including groceries, dry goods, and hardware. It also handled goods being sent down the St Lawrence for export. By the 1840s it was receiving more goods from overseas than any other firm in the city.

Typical of merchants of the time, Moffatt had a hand in many enterprises other than his own, including the Lower Canada Land Company, the British American Land Company, the Phoenix Fire Assurance Company, and the Champlain and St Lawrence Railroad. He was also a large landowner. Like other Anglo-Scottish merchants who helped maintain Montreal's commercial hegemony in the 1840s, Moffatt seemed able to profit from each opportunity as it came along whether it was furs, wheat, manufactures, insurance, railways, or land speculation. Many of the merchants were active in politics and used their appointed or elected offices to promote their own commercial interests as well as those of Montreal.

latest agricultural periodicals from England or the United States; in the evening they can sit by the fire with the latest novel by Dickens – probably in one of the pirated American editions that so anger the author. All of this has contributed to the expansive, "improving" mood of the English and, although not always articulated, to their deeper instincts for anglicizing those they brush up against. They have completely absorbed the Dutch of New Amsterdam and are even now pushing back the last frontiers of Irish and Gaelic at home. Would not the French Canadians benefit from the same experience?

Certainly, many of the supporters of the 1841 union presume so. For them, the designation of English as the sole language of the United Assembly makes good sense; so, too, does the choice of an Upper Canadian city, Kingston, as the capital. French-Canadian legislators will be forced to leave their narrow little world along the St Lawrence and will be exposed to the superiority of a British institution that, no doubt, will inspire emulation. Upper-class French Canadians are most likely to take on English ways first. Indeed, many are already fluent in English and it seemed to Lord Durham, during his brief stay, that this class had already "adopted some English customs and feelings." Forming another bridge between the two peoples, they, like others before them, have found that bridges are frequently stepped on – from both sides. This is particularly true at election time. Voting is open and lasts for several days, providing plenty of opportunity for intimidation and abuse. Take, for example, the elderly French Canadian who, being too ill to walk, came to the hustings in Quebec's Upper Town in a cariole to vote in the 1841 election. When he supported the two union candidates, he was, according to the *Quebec Mercury,* insulted with the most hideous yells and other noises" that could be heard from the market nearby. This "naturally called forth three hearty cheers from those who approved of his vote." When the polls closed several days later, it was found that the unionist candidates had won.

The Upper Town market might bustle with British soldiers, immigrants, and government officials, but a few steps away, behind the plain exterior of the French cathedral, the old world goes on much as it always has. None of the din of the market can penetrate the thick walls, although the smell of horses and stale tobacco does tag along on the clothing of the worshipers. During the quiet periods when no services are taking place, there are always a few persons – often in working clothes – sitting silently in the pews apparently doing nothing. Over here, a man might be staring upwards with fixed eyes as he whispers his prayers so quickly that he must gasp for air: over there, another might be cooly muttering to himself, stopping every now and then for a pinch of snuff or to spit. At one

The French cathedral.
*Detail from **The Market Place, Quebec** by W.H. Bartlett.*
*In Willis, **Canadian Scenery**, vol. 2, facing p. 11*

side is the confessional, where a well-dressed lady or an Indian with long black hair might be seen kneeling with mouth pressed to the lattice-work on one side or the other of the box. In the dim light, it is just possible to make out the dark form of the priest as he slowly moves back and forth from one lattice to the other. Like other French-Canadian churches, the highly ornamented interior makes "a show of glory" in shimmering contrast with the chaste exterior. All is white plaster, gilt-work, brightly painted statues, pictures with crimson curtains, and grey wax candles, five feet tall or more. On entering or leaving, it is the practice to dip into the holy water at the door and make the sign of the cross. Some of the leading priests come from France, but most are drawn from various segments of Canadian society. The priesthood provides one of the few opportunities for social advancement. Through it, a bright boy from a poor family might gain an education and social standing in his community.

A spirit of renewal is sweeping the Canadian church as the new decade dawns: greater effort is being made than ever before to confirm the wavering in their faith and to bring new converts into the fold. That these efforts are unusually successful is due, in part, to religious retreats. These resemble somewhat the religious revival meetings now so popular among the Protestants in English Canada and in the United States. In Upper Canada, newspapers are buzzing with tales of the excesses said to be taking place – especially among the youth – at revival meetings that are often held in remote locations back in the forest. Such talk was less likely to arise during the week-long retreat held in the Quebec cathedral in the fall of 1840. There, religious fervour was rekindled in separate meetings – one for men only, another for women – conducted each day by a conservative preacher of extraordinary power, Monseigneur de Forbin-Janson, the former bishop of Nancy in France. Those taking part gave themselves up wholly to confessions, penances, fastings, and prayer, by which they obtain absolution for the past and indulgences for the future. Throughout the whole day, there was hardly an interval of five minutes when a person could not be seen entering or leaving the cathedral. Most of the participants had come from the French suburbs or the surrounding villages. More than 4000 could be accommodated in the cathedral at one time. Buckingham thought the appearance of the worshipers was exactly like that of the peasantry on a feast day in any of the provinces of northern France, although with somewhat less of the hilarity and with a more subdued tone of dress and manners.

Respectable society at Quebec is composed of the civil and military officials, seigneurs, professional men, the two bishops and the clergy, and, until recently, the viceregal court. Society in the other Canadian cities – Montreal, Kingston, and Toronto – does not differ greatly from that of Quebec. None of these remote little cities – Montreal, the largest, is only 40,000 – can be described as the *dernier cri* of the fashionable world: visitors from abroad have been unkind enough to compare them with second- or third-rate provincial towns in England or France, yet this does not prevent their respectable citizens from affecting the pretensions of metropolitan society. A stranger among them is met with the most hospitable attention, provided he is properly introduced, but the grades of classification into which society is divided could place him in a situation that is far from pleasant. He might soon discover that his rank in Canada depends not so much on his character or on the society among which he lived before coming to Canada, as on the accident of introduction. Should he be unlucky enough to carry an introduction to, or associate with on arrival, a family that does not visit the governor's residence, he will be shunned by all of the elite, especially the ladies, as long as he lives in Canada.

Such pretensions strike many visitors to Canada as laughable and ridiculous. Among the harshest observers is Anna Jameson, whose unhappy marriage brought her to live in Toronto. Although not above complaining herself, she was struck by the number of "repining and discontented women" she saw in Canada. Indeed, she "never met with *one* woman recently settle here, who considered herself happy in her new home and country," although she had "*heard* of one." It seemed to her that those who were "really accomplished" and accustomed to the "best society" managed better than those "whose claim to social distinction could not have been great anywhere" and whom she "found lamenting over themselves, as if they had been so many exiled princesses." Those who had been brought up in Canada were quite different, however, and "many of them had adopted a sort of pride in their new country ... there was always a great desire to visit England, and some little airs of self-complacency and superiority in those who had been there, though for a few months only; but all, without a single exception, returned with pleasure, unable to forego the early habitual influences of their native land."

Of all the influences that set apart those born in Canada from their cousins brought up in the old country, probably none is more striking than the "levelling influence" so often commented upon by British visitors. Upper-class pretensions aside, this open society is felt by all North Americans, whether they be in the United States – where it is said to be most extreme – or in the more class-conscious British colonies. Some visitors from the old country are astonished

"We were rather entertained by the behaviour of a young Scotchman, the engineer of the steamer, on my husband addressing him with reference to the management of the engine. His manners were surly, and almost insolent. He scrupulously avoided the least approach to courtesy or outward respect; nay, he even went so far as to seat himself on the bench close beside me, and observed that among the many advantages this country offered to settlers like him, he did not reckon it the least of them that he was not obliged to take off his hat when he spoke to people (meaning persons of our degree), or address them by any other title than their name; besides, he could go and take his seat beside any gentleman or lady either, and think himself to the full as good as them."

Catherine Parr Traill, *Backwoods of Canada*, 83–4

to discover that those whom they had always considered their social inferiors suddenly expected to be treated as equals; others are delighted to find they no longer have to kowtow to those above them, and insolently revel in their new-found independence. In the new world, one does not hire a "maid" or a "farm-servant" but rather a "girl" or a "man," who becomes almost a member of the family, even eating at table with the "master" or "mistress." Such behaviour has drawn shocked comment from those who retain their old-world social presumptions. On occasion, even *they* find themselves in the disagreeable position of being forced to sit at a common table in some country inn or on board a steamship.

There is something quintessentially American about mealtime on board the United States Great Lakes steamers. Food is super-abundant and every dish is spread out on the table at the beginning of the meal. Persons of all ranks sit crowded around it, their long arms concentrating on their own needs as they quickly empty the white china cramming every inch of the table. All this is disagreeable to the English traveller, who prefers the more civilized arrangements on steamers from the British side of the lakes where meals are served one course at a time on fine, patterned English china. Still there is a grudging respect for small signs of American ingenuity, such as keeping the butter firm by serving it with ice.

The common table, or *table d'hôte*, is also the usual arrangement in Canadian hotels. Perhaps this has come about because so many of the proprietors are Americans. So, too, are many of the guests – often merchants, or travellers doing the Northern Tour through the northern states and Canada. Hotels in towns and cities along the tour route are said to offer superior accommodation. Montreal, for instance, has benefited by being near Saratoga Springs, a favourite watering place in upper New York State.

American and Upper Canadian hotel guests have a reputation for being excessively inquisitive, causing some English guests to arrange to take their meals in their rooms. This might spare them the pain of being plagued with questions about where they have come from, how they like the country, what their fathers did, what their wives are like, and so on; but it also might prevent them from picking up some serviceable information about the country, along with astonishingly minute accounts of the lives and future prospects of their informants. Yet, even had they chosen to do so, picking up this information might not have been easy. Over the years, the language of England and America has diverged along separate paths. Two decades ago, one visitor put it well when he described the American language as an "old friend with a new face."

Canadian speech is also quite different and it is not uncommon for the newly arrived to mistake an English Canadian for an American. It is remarkable how quickly immigrants – whether from England, Scotland, Ireland, Germany, or Holland – adopt the speech, manners, and customs of North America. Upper-class Englishmen have assumed that this rapid transition has something to do with the fact that migrants generally come from the lowest ranks of society and that as soon as they arrive in Canada they take on an appearance of importance and become quite ashamed of their former unassuming manners and native customs. They quickly join the older residents in decrying the dialects and customs of their former homelands. What can be more degrading than the newly imported English immigrant affecting yankee airs? The genuine yankee might have his points, but the bad imitation is always worse than the original. Surely, he should "glory in the title of *Englishman,* and esteem it as much a privilege as ever did the Roman that of *Citizen,*" and "carry with him to the colony the manners, habits, and principles of the mother country." But this is not the case. Instead, the English Canadian copies "the worse and most prominent features of the American character, and the British settler in turn caricatured the copy." As the national character of the people gradually slips away, there is an increasing danger that the colony might amalgamate with the United States.

What is needed are British settlers of the better class who, by precept and example, will foster a love for the British institutions of the colony. These virtues can be found in the British middle class – the class for which Britain is becoming increasingly celebrated abroad, and the class that is sorely under-represented in Canada. Voltaire compared the component parts of British society with their favourite beverage, beer: the top or higher orders was all froth, the bottom or poorer class was all dregs, but the middle was excellent. It is this portion of society – with its virtuous principle, moral order, and superior intelligence – that Canada sorely needs. Yet in 1841 the Canadian middle class remains small and, to a large extent, those possessing entrepreneurial skills are largely drawn from the United States. "Jonathan," as the American is known, is pictured as "shrewd and calculating" and is renowned for "driving a hard bargain" and for his "zeal and industry." While these qualities evoke a furtive admiration on the part of the British, there is also a fear that Jonathan might introduce among the other settlers "that extreme spirit of democracy," which can not fail but be attended with unpleasant consequences.

To the newly arrived Englishmen, attuned to a land where a man's speech immediately revealed his rank and locality of origin, Canada is a confusing place: not only is he never certain whether a person is an English Canadian or an American, but he also has difficulty in assigning a precise degree of social rank. For instance, labourers receive higher wages than at home and are consequently more closely united with the wealthy who, themselves, frequently spring from the labouring ranks. In the countryside, the lines of society are further blurred by the custom of working in "bees." Here, it is not at all unusual to see a retired half-pay officer, stripped to the waist, labouring shoulder to shoulder with an Irish navvy. Shopkeepers can be another source of confusion. Not only do they keep the general store in the community but they also assume the role of merchant, banker, and, not infrequently, of magistrate, commissioner, or, even, member of the provincial parliament. The newcomer might well be surprised to discover standing behind the counter the son of a clergyman or of a military or naval officer. According to Catherine Parr Trail, they do not "lose their grade in society by such employment."

After all, she muses hopefully, it is "education and manners that must distinguish the gentlemen in this country." The labouring man, if he is diligent and industrious, might soon become his equal in point of worldly possession; however, the ignorant man, "let him be ever so wealthy, can never be equal to the man of education. It is the mind that forms the distinction between the classes in this country." Sir Richard Bonneycastle, commander of the Royal Engineers in Upper Canada during the late rebellions, is in agreement and notes that in Montreal "in the countinghouses ... the advantages of situation and education made the same differences as in other countries." The mind may form the distinction between the classes but the differences are usually underlined by the choice of distinctive clothing. In St James Street there is no mistaking the man from the countinghouse in his frock coat and top hat. Yet, grand though he might seem as he picks his way along the filthy street, he is no match for the birds of passage in military uniforms.

Soldiers in brilliant scarlet, black, and gold have captured the eye of the visiting artist – many of whom are themselves in the military – and few can resist placing two or three lounging officers or men in the foreground of their sketches and watercolours. Garrisons are to be found in most towns and cities and it is the presence of so many soldiers that provides the most striking difference between street scenes in Canada and in the United States or Great Britain.

Soldier in scarlet. Detail from **The Rideau Canal, Bytown** *by W.H. Bartlett. In Willis,* **Canadian Scenery,** *vol. 2, after p. 6*

At Quebec there is one soldier for every eighteen or nineteen civilians; at Montreal, perhaps one for every twenty-three or twenty-four. Similar numbers can be found at other strategic points in Canada: St John's, Prescott, Bytown, Kingston, Toronto, and Niagara.

The Toronto garrison has its headquarters in the rather poor barracks that are so agreeably situated on the lakefront about a mile and a half west of the city – a pleasant jaunt for the notables of the place when they set out to pay a formal call after each new regiment takes up residence. Shortly after such visits, invitations are received by the officers and, before long, they find themselves filling the comfortable niches in Toronto society that had been vacated by their predecessors when they were transferred to some other part of the empire. As elsewhere in Canada, the way has been smoothed by the enchantment of the regimental band which, in Toronto, gives concerts twice a week. (During the early weeks of summer, the tormented musicians must glance with hidden envy at their listeners – after all, they have both hands free to defend themselves against the detachments of invading mosquitoes.)

The numerous American tourists who arrive each summer flock to hear the regimental bands. There is a nice irony in the fact that the very soldiers who have been sent out at enormous expense to discourage an invasion from the south have actually become an enticement. Everywhere brother Jonathan and his family can be seen hurrying from the steamboats to the parade squares and the various military emplacements, including the Citadel at Quebec. Military exercises such as those carried out on the Plains of Abraham are very popular. On one such occasion the American ladies were described by one of the officers as being "well dressed ... and very pretty – showing no silly timidity but great good sense and courage during the firing."

Tourists browsing in Quebec's Upper Town market are often "caught by the ears" by a band leaving the nearby Jesuit Barracks on its way to the governor's residence for the regular changing of the Castle Guard. For those living in Quebec, and in other Canadian cities as well, bands are so commonplace as to be hardly noticed: no important person can arrive or depart without a musical salute; no soirée, ball, or steamship excursion is complete without a band; even touring singers share the stage with a military band; and each day ends with the roll of drums at the beating of the tattoo, signaling that the time has come to leave the taverns and fleshpots and return to the crowded barracks with their noisome urine barrels.

Even more important than the bands in establishing good relations between garrison and town is the aid freely given by the military in times of emergency resulting from fire, disease, or natural disaster. When part of the Quebec rock broke away and came crashing down into the houses in Champlain Street in May 1841, the military of the garrison were promptly on the spot and operations began to rescue those trapped beneath the rubble. (Twenty-two were saved, but at least thirty-two died in the tragedy.) Six months later, during a freezing November night, the post office in the Upper Town burned to the ground. Had it not been for the military, including the artillerymen who worked the fire-engine, the flames would have spread from building to building until stopped by some

27

1, 2
The First or
Grenadier
Regiment of Foot
Guards.
1: captain;
2: private.
Metropolitan
Toronto
Reference Library,
J. Ross Robertson
Collection,
1465

3, 4
Regiment of Cold
Stream Guards.
3: captain;
4: private.
Metropolitan
Toronto
Reference Library,
J. Ross Robertson
Collection,
1533

open space that placed other structures beyond their reach. Unfortunately, this is the usual pattern followed by fires in this crowded city of narrow streets.

In 1841 battalions of two of Britain's most celebrated regiments are stationed at Quebec – the Grenadier and the Coldstream guards. They came out in 1838 in response to the rebellions. Among the officers are members of some well-known English families, including Robert Peel Dawson, nephew of Sir Robert Peel. There is insufficient room for officers in the barracks and, with hotel and other accommodation being both scarce and expensive, Dawson has been forced to share a garret, up three flights of stairs, with a fellow officer – and with numerous bedbugs. Most of the houses rented or owned by officers are in the St Louis Street area. From time to time advertisements for the sale of furniture and other possessions of departing officers give an indication of the very comfortable life some of them enjoy in Canada. Dawson brought over his "Mamma's fur coat," which alone has prevented him "from being chilled to death" during guard duty at the Citadel. Like other officers, Dawson has had a great deal of leisure time for balls, dinners, theatricals, horse races, sleigh rides, various sports, reading, sketching, and attending the officers' mess with its rituals and strict code of behaviour. The ordinary men, of course, endure a very different existence.

With only 6 per cent of the soldiers permitted to take their wives overseas at government expense, most of the troops live single lives – accounting, in part, for the large number of taverns and brothels in Quebec. (The brothels are concentrated in the St Johns suburb.)

Not surprisingly, there are many brawls among the men, some involving the civilian population. Yet, here, as elsewhere in the empire, perceptions of the common soldier are changing: like the poor, the criminal, and the insane, he is now capable of transformation. Attendance at certain public lectures and plays is being encouraged, and attempts are even made to convince him of the worthiness of the temperance cause. At the same time, a number of the more onerous fatigue duties, such as the emptying of latrines, are being eliminated through contracting them out to civilians. Most of the soldiers (and many of the wives and children) live in barracks – some dating back to the French period – but others are billeted in the city, within the walls of the Upper Town.

In 1836 the military headquarters were moved to Montreal, thus giving Montreal precedence over Quebec and the other garrison towns. Soldiers are everywhere to be seen in Montreal, but the belles of the town know that the most fashionable military walk is Notre Dame Street. From the corners of their downcast eyes, demure ladies catch glimpses of the Grenadier with his tall hat or the Hussar on horseback with his jacket jauntily hanging from the shoulder. Who knows, she might end up beside one of these officers in a handsome carriage or in a sleigh behind the bobbed tail of one of the beautiful horses some of them own. (Officers' horses are apparently accorded the deference due to their masters: at the run-down artillery quarters on LaCroix Street, a cook house separates the stalls for the officers' horses from those of lesser rank.) Officers are under orders not to marry while on colonial service. Girls who become too involved are in danger of sharing the fate of the Misses Billings and Roberts, who were left in tears on Brown's Wharf at Toronto when the 34th Regiment sailed for England on 22 May 1841.

Desertion is common – and no doubt women are involved in many cases. The soldier's lot is never easy but in North America it contrasts sharply with the offhand ways of the "levelling system." Many of the garrisons are near the American border. Once a soldier has slipped across, it is easy for him to blend in with other migrants from the British Isles. There is little about the deserter that might betray his past except, perhaps, his lack of success as a settler: years of regimentation often robbed him of that flexibility of mind so necessary for success on the frontier. Temptation is especially great along the Niagara River where everything, even the farm animals, seems to be bigger and better on the far side of the river. On one occasion several desperate deserters drowned in attempting to swim across and, for weeks afterwards, their bloated bodies could be seen eerily circling round and round in the whirlpool below the falls, their arms moving as if swimming.

To the British soldier, Canada consists of sweltering through an Italian summer in a woollen uniform that is too heavy or in shivering through a Russian winter, inadequately clothed. During the coldest months at Quebec, the sentries are changed every hour. As

they hurry to and from their posts their bayonets are not fixed – probably to prevent them from impaling themselves, or some innocent civilian, should they slip on the ice. Once at their posts, bayonets must be in place and, no matter how severe the weather, sentries are not to leave their muskets "on any pretence whatever" for longer than is absolutely necessary for levelling the path after every drift or fall of snow. There have been instances of soldiers who have dropped or mislaid their mittens and had their hands frostbitten while holding their muskets. Officers carry little pocket mirrors to check their faces from time to time to see if there are any telltale signs of frostbite. If there are, the recommended treatment is the "speedy application of friction and snow [to] restore the dormant action, and prevent putrefaction which would otherwise ensue."

The soldier freezing at Quebec may well have sweltered in India or Jamaica during an earlier posting. They may be birds of passage, yet they bring with them an element of excitement from exotic far-away places. What money they have they spend freely, and it passes through many hands after leaving the taverns and shops. The officers are often quite well off and have added considerably to the wealth of the place. Many of their skills, in fields such as engineering and medicine, have directly benefited the country through the construction of roads and canals, through geological exploration, and in providing aid during epidemics. They have also given their time to many charities and organizations ranging from friendly societies to literary and historical organizations. The content of the papers presented by the officers to the latter organizations shows that many of them have been caught up in the "improving spirit" that is now sweeping the British Isles and the United States.

Some officers have chosen on retirement to settle in Canada on half-pay. Because of their superior education and "other means," half-pay officers have not been above assuming the role of "country gentlemen." Usually they are in a better position to take risks and experiment with new techniques in agriculture, as well as to provide leadership to the wider community, than are most of their neighbours, who generally exist on the edge of subsistence during their early years in Canada.

"Our society is mostly military or naval," Catherine Parr Traill wrote in her recent account of life in the backwoods of Upper Canada. "We meet on equal grounds, and are, of course, well acquainted with the rules of good breeding and polite life; too much so to allow any deviation from those laws that good taste, good sense, and good feeling have established among persons of our class." As a "bush-lady," Mrs Traill does not care what others think of her when she performs her own household tasks and even milks her own cows, for she knows that "as a British officer must needs be a gentleman and his wife a lady, perhaps we repose quietly on that incontestable proof of our gentility." One does have to maintain standards, though, and her servants are not "admitted to our tables, or placed on an equality with us, excepting at 'bees,' and such kinds of public meetings."

Pretentious English gentlefolk like the Traills fascinated Robertson and one can detect the irony in his voice as he sympathized with their difficulties in keeping up appearances. The Traills's fear of losing status was one of their reasons for emigrating to Canada. They were by no means alone in this. Sons of small-scale farmers, for instance, saw in emigration a means to avoid sinking to the rank of day labourers. Others saw emigration as a means of holding their families together; still others saw in it an acceptable way to flee family responsibilities or, perhaps, of ending an unhappy affair. Greater independence was a strong underlying motive. So, too, was an opportunity to escape from escalating rents, taxes, and tithes – not to mention an overbearing master. Nor should a spirit of adventure and an underlying faith in subsistence farming be overlooked. Any one of these motivations was enough to draw some of the most unlikely emigrants to Canada. Many somehow managed to survive but others moved on, leaving behind little more than an overgrown clearing, a few rotting logs, and a pile of stones where the chimney had been.

Chapter Two

The
Rage
of
Emigration

Robertson's interest in emigration, particularly from the Scottish Highlands, can be traced back to his youthful friendship with Lord Selkirk. His early idealism and enthusiasm was tempered over the years as he learned more about the conditions at the ports of embarkation, the horrendous passages on the emigrant ships, and the many hardships faced by the settlers when they arrived in Canada. He was particularly chagrined about the fate of Selkirk's Red River settlers, since he had provided them with encouragement to emigrate to the Canadian Northwest. All of this is reflected in the tone of this fragment, which he had entitled "the rage of emigration." It is filled with the caution and the admonitions of a man well along in his years.

Although Robertson was never on board an emigrant ship, he had witnessed these vessels leaving from Greenock and had seen them arriving in Quebec. During his tour of the Canadas in the summer of 1841 he visited the emigrant sheds and hospitals in the various ports along his route. He was particularly touched by the poor, disillusioned migrants he came upon at Kingston, who were trying to survive by breaking rocks in a government make-work project.

Robertson was the victim of a peculiar type of arthritis known as "Edinburgh knee," which prevented him from straying far from the steamship routes. For the most part he was forced to resort to second-hand accounts for information about conditions along the frontier in the interior. On the steamers and in the inns he took every opportunity to speak to newly arrived emigrants – exhausted yet brimming with excitement – and with disillusioned and downcast settlers on their way out again to the "front."

*T*he very prosperity of Canada depends on the immigrant feeling welcome and wanted in the colony. If he is unhappy with his reception he will simply leave, probably for the United States, and let people back home know his unfavourable thoughts of the country. If he is well received, however, he will write back to his friends and relatives and the flow of immigrants will be further increased. This undoubtedly will be the case when news of a group of 270 Highland Scots reaches the Isle of Lewis from the Eastern Townships of Lower Canada, where they arrived late in 1841 to join some of their countrymen who had settled in the Townships three years ago.

So poor are the Highlanders that when they left Scotland they carried only a few possessions and a little oatmeal for the voyage. When they arrived at Quebec they did not even have enough money to pay the carters for the removal of their luggage. Since then, they have been sustained largely through the generosity of the people of Lower Canada. When they finally reached their fellow countrymen in the bush there was a generous outpouring of Highland hospitality. Without hesitation, the old settlers were sharing the provisions they had laid in for the winter and were taking into their cramped huts as many as twenty newcomers. Meanwhile, collections are being made in Montreal and Sherbrooke through the St Andrew's society. A number of snug log cabins are being prepared and plans are afoot to furnish each man with an axe, and to procure a few kettles and other cooking utensils to be used in common in the settlement. As the year 1841 ended, a good many of the girls and boys had managed to find employment in the Townships – in spite of their speaking only Gaelic. Their small wages will help the community get through the first difficult winter and on to the next step towards prosperity. Those who came out three years earlier, with scarcely a single exception, are doing well. A considerable amount of forest has been cleared and sufficient crops are being raised to sustain the little colony in comfort. Indeed, it was reports of the settlers' prosperous condition in letters to Scotland that had brought out the new arrivals.

Emigration is now generally accepted as being beneficial to the mother country as well as to the colonies. The British Isles are becoming overcrowded and, by reducing the number of mouths to feed, there is more scope for those who remain behind. By sending people to the colonies, markets for British products are being enlarged and work is being created for her manufacturers and artisans at home. To convey these goods, the merchant fleet will necessarily expand and this, in turn, will provide trained seamen to fight her battles in times of peril. Yet, in spite of emigration, the population of the British Isles continues to grow and there is in some quarters an inkling that the more enterprising and industrious are leaving while the "idle and dissolute" are remaining at home.

Who should emigrate? Guide books such as Evans's *The Emigrant's Directory and Guide* are blunt in telling *"the idler, the drunkard,* or the *seditious"* that he "must abandon his vicious practices and habits ... before he can expect to succeed in Canada." Doyle's *Hints on Emigration* is equally frank when it discourages "mere adventurers – broken down tradesmen, and scheming shopkeepers" from going overseas, and candidly adds that they might "just as well stay and starve quietly at home – such persons would not prosper any where." Doyle also cautions ladies and gentlemen of *very small* means to stay at home, since they are generally too tenderly reared "to dispense with the services of domestics, whom they could not afford to pay in a country where a good pair of hands is worth much." An exception might be "the families of naval or military gentlemen accustomed to *rough it,* habituated to discipline and self control, and possessed of adequate zeal and energy."

In some communities, especially in Ireland and the Scottish Highlands, desperate people are being caught up in "the rage of emigration." In the valleys and glens, and in villages along the coast, they can be seen loading their meager possessions into carts and heading towards gathering places such as Cork and Tobermory. From there, either they will sail directly to Canada or, as is more likely, they will sail first to a larger port like Greenock, Liverpool, or London and then transfer to a transatlantic ship. In either case, it means a heart-wrenching departure, for they know that the handshake at the ship-side is the handshake of the death bed.

Lists are readily available of what to take on board. On ships sailing from Scotland and Ireland, it is customary for passengers to carry their own provisions. Should these run out, the poor passengers are forced to buy (at extortionate prices) from the captain, who always happens to have an extra supply on hand. In addition, all passengers should carry what they can afford in the way of goods and supplies for starting life in a new and unfamiliar land. Besides the usual household utensils, less familiar items such as logging chains of Swedish iron for use with oxen should be packed. British axes should be left behind because they are likely to shatter in the cold Canadian climate. It is also a good idea to bring along a wife, since there is a surplus of men in Canada and an over supply of women in Great Britain. Besides, a man will find a woman of his own country more congenial to his habits and taste – at least, so it is said.

There is always a great deal of confusion in the ports and many of the emigrants are the innocent victims of fraud. Runners are everywhere, directing them to decrepit ships and flea-bitten boarding houses. A vessel might be listed as AE. 1 – the E indicating an old ship – but the E might be so tiny that the would-be passenger would mistake the ship as being A. 1. Sailing dates are not often adhered to, causing a loss of valuable time and the wasting of much of the small savings of the emigrants, who are forced to pay for accommodation at the port. Many of the boats bound for Quebec are timber ships, usually in ballast and not always the most pleasant or the safest description of transport. There are laws governing the amount of space per passenger, provisions to be carried, and matters of health and safety, but these are by no means always obeyed.

Most of the passengers who arrived late in the season last year had been at sea for ten to fourteen weeks – usually after waiting one to four weeks at the port of embarkation. The differences in sailing times was accounted for by differing weather conditions and the quality of the various ships. The longer the trip, the more likely provisions had deteriorated or even run out and, of course, the more likely the passengers had been ill – necessitating a stay at the quarantine station on arrival. Those who survived – and some did not – arrived penniless in Quebec or Montreal in August or September, too late to go up country to settle. Early in 1841 some of these late arrivals were still to be seen begging in the streets – their only means of support during the long winter.

Regardless of when the ships set out from Britain, there is a tendency for them to group together in the lower St Lawrence, awaiting favourable winds to take them up river against the current. This can result in a spectacular scene such as that which occurred one day during the third week of May this year when, from down river, there suddenly appeared a huge flotilla of ships coming up on an east wind. People on the new Durham Terrace near the château counted no fewer than 112 vessels at one time. More ships quickly followed and, by the fourth day, 313 ships filled the harbour. Most of them were in ballast and would return loaded with timber. Some like the *Sara Botsford*, which had sailed from Glasgow on 20 April, carried general cargo and 222 passengers. Among them were a large number of hand weavers connected with the Calton Emigration Society who were seeking a better life in Canada. With 520 passengers, the *Marchioness Abercorn* carried, by far, the largest number of immigrants in the fleet. She had sailed from Londonderry on 23 April. Both of these ships had made very good time. So, too, had the *Minstrel* from Limerick, but as she came up the St Lawrence she struck a reef. Altogether, 137 passengers (eighty-eight adults and forty-nine children) and eleven crewmen were drowned. Only four crewmen and four passengers survived. (Later in the summer, forty-one more people perished when another ship from Limerick, the *Amanda,* went down off Metis.)

Overall, 7047 passengers had arrived in only a few days – 5313 from Ireland, 1241 from England, and 488 from Scotland. The remaining five were from the lower ports. This is nearly double the number who had arrived by the same date the previous year – a very encouraging sign that the country is on the mend.

It is always tempting for the newly arrived immigrant to stop over for a few days in Quebec and Montreal to regain his land legs. This, however, is unwise since it means throwing away the most valuable days of the year. Far better to move on to one's destination as quickly as possible in order to accomplish as much as can possibly be done during the short summer in preparation for the rigours of the long Canadian winter.

From the river, Montreal can seem very enticing. Most of the buildings within the city proper are of stone, giving an impression of great solidity. On closer inspection, the dark stone used in the construction and the iron shutters on many of the windows evoke a sense of depression and gloominess. In the suburbs, many of the buildings are of wood. The streets are in general wretchedly paved, full of deep holes and ruts. Because of the soft limestone used, even the macadamized streets are very muddy when wet and very dusty when dry. The skyline is dominated by the roofs and steeples of the many religious institutions, both Roman Catholic and Protestant. The largest is the new Catholic Cathedral of Notre Dame – perhaps the largest church in North America. It can accommodate 10,000 persons at once, nearly half the Catholics of Montreal.

Montreal is now the main commercial centre of the Canadas. It has been for some years but it was only in the past decade that it

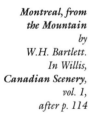

Montreal, from the Mountain by *W.H. Bartlett. In Willis,* **Canadian Scenery,** *vol. 1, after p. 114*

edged out Quebec as the country's largest city. Montreal's population is about 40,000. Immigrants land near the warehouses which are filled with the latest manufactures from Great Britain as well as the exotic produce of the West Indies and the East Indies. Much of this is destined for the upper province. The warehouses also hold the produce of the upper country and the neighbouring areas of the United States that wait export to Europe.

In the city and neighbourhood can be seen examples of most of the manufacturing industries found in the Canadas – tanning, hatting, leather dressing, soap and candle making, nail making, rope making, and ship building. Skilled immigrants *might* find work here. There are also the unmistakable odours associated with breweries, distilleries, foundries, and furriers. Large quantities of pork and beef from the United States are salted for export. The timber trade is important, even though many rafts are floated past the city down to Quebec. The produce seen in the well-stocked markets is mostly from the Island of Montreal, and from farms along the south shore and the Eastern Townships.

Like Montreal, Kingston presents a very striking appearance from the water. But unlike Montreal, whose island is known as "the Garden of Canada," the rocky land immediately about Kingston is not very suitable for agriculture. The little city of seven or eight thousand is trying hard to live up to its new role as the Canadian metropolis. Pianos and other emblems of metropolitanism are being imported but the sight of scavenging pigs and poultry seen from parlour windows diminishes somewhat the new air of sophistication. In the broad streets, including the high street, it is still possible to feed one's horse on the grass growing down the centre – provided the roaming cows have not cropped it too short. For the

View to the south along King St from the R.D. Cartwright house. Kingston, Ontario, 1833-34. Pen and brown ink over pencil drawing on wove paper by Harriet Cartwright. NAC

more prosperous residents of the town, several brand new cabs have been brought in. As they jog along the rocky streets with their well-dressed passengers, they pass many pathetically poor and destitute persons, especially in the area around the immigrant sheds near the wharves, the driver all the while keeping a sharp eye out for the many drunks lying on the ground in the final stages of intoxication. Such contrasts between those in extreme poverty and those making showy attempts "to imitate real wealth and grandeur" can be jarring.

Kingston is said to be busy "making hay while the sun shines." There are great speculations in real estate, and new buildings are springing up everywhere – some in anticipation of the city's new role, others as replacements for those burned in the great fire of last year. Immigrants are cautioned that wages, rents, provisions and board are rising, and all too common is the experience of a stonemason who returned to Kingston from the western part of the province to take advantage of the building boom, only to discover that no "apartment of any description" could be found within three miles of the city. Even accommodation for gentlemen is scarce, and some of those being forced to move to the new capital have found themselves "in situations scarcely better than that of a drove of emigrants on shipboard," according to the jaundiced *Morning Courier* of Montreal: "Bedrooms that were never intended to hold more than one human carcass have aspired and been voted worthy of the honour of receiving half a dozen, whilst closets and corners hitherto quietly resigned to the rats and cockroaches, have echoed to the somniferous snoring of wearied and almost grateful politicians."

The Toronto newspapers have also had harsh things to say about Kingston. Yet, in many ways, especially in matters of strength, beauty, and convenience, Kingston has an edge on Toronto, even though it lacks its rival's surroundings of rich agricultural land. In spite of Kingston's obvious advantages, however, it already seems possible that the shortsightedness of its business gentry might jeopardize the city's future promise as the capital of the Canadas.

Toronto is the final port of call for many emigrants. It is here they obtain what supplies they can afford before heading inland to the new settlements along the frontier, thus allowing the merchants of the place to cream off what little money the emigrant might possess. From the city they may take one of several roads that lead into the peninsula of Upper Canada. On their way, they may pass produce from newly established farms moving in to Toronto, where it will add to the wealth of the city. As the population in the back country increases and prospers, so too do the merchants, manufacturers, and tradesmen of Toronto who supply the settlers' needs and buy their produce. The city is now the main banking and financial centre of Upper Canada.

Stretching along the lakeshore and backed by magnificent pine

forests, Toronto presents a charming picture to those arriving by boat. But there is much truth in the old adage of distance lending enchantment. The hands being waved on shore, the disembarking passengers soon discover, were more likely to have beeen raised against swarms of mosquitoes and flies than in friendly greeting. The cheerful peeping heard on board turns out to be a plague of frogs that disturbs the sleep at night – sleep that is also disrupted by fleas and bedbugs. The few imposing buildings seen from the harbour – including the parliament house, hospital, college, and jail – on closer inspection have little architectural merit.

View in King Street (Looking Eastward), City of Toronto, Upper Canada by T. Young, stone by J.H. Bufford, lithograph by N. Currier, NAC

Torontonians are quick to point out to the disappointed new-comer all the improvements which have taken place in their home town of 15,000 during the short seven years since it was incorporated and had its name changed from York to Toronto. No longer can people across the lake derisively compare "Little York," the capital of Upper Canada, with New York, "the greatest emporium in America." The new municipal government has done so much to improve the notorious condition of the streets – streets long famed for mud-holes that "yawned to engulf the jolting wagon" and crossings abounding in unfathomable puddles "which would slip off your Wellingtons like a boot-jack." Some of the main streets are now paved or macadamized, miles of plank sidewalks have been laid – the boards being placed lengthwise as on a ship's deck – and a general system of draining is being installed.

TORONTO MERCHANTS

Among the most successful Toronto merchants in 1841 was Isaac Buchanan. Born in Scotland and well educated, he had been able to profit from family business connections in the old country as well as from access to capital from his Glasgow bank. Like many merchants, he was active in politics and in 1841 narrowly won a Toronto seat in the Legislative Assembly for the reformers. Perhaps more typical was Yorkshireman Thomas Thompson who, like Buchanan, had arrived in Canada in 1830. He first opened a school, which prospered and allowed him to enter the retail trade. His "Thomas Thompson's Cheap Shoe Store" is said to have been the first boot store in Toronto. Soon this shrewd, lean man with the deep-set eyes and side whiskers added dry goods, clothing, and millinery to his stock. Meanwhile, his school was sold to other immigrants who wished to get established in the same way. At the mouth of the Don stood the mill of yet another thriving merchant, William Gooderham. In 1837 he added a distillery to his enterprise to make more efficient use of surplus and second-grade grain. By 1841 he was able to introduce gas lighting and convert the plant to steam power. All three were characteristic of the merchants of the 1840s. Buchanan eventually failed and went bankrupt, a not uncommon outcome at that time; Thompson passed his business to a son; and Gooderham's enterprise continued to prosper long after he was gone.

Toronto property values are said to be "incredible" and "many persons who were formerly very needy are now amongst the richest." In spite of the confusion and depression since the Rebellions of 1837–38, the city has continued to grow and prosper. However, now that the capital has moved to Kingston there is fear all this might change; the Toronto *Patriot* has predicted that property values might drop by as much as 25 and 30 per cent.

Toronto, like Montreal and Kingston, is filled with hazards to health and morals – not to mention the pocketbook. The finely dressed "gentleman" who approaches the unwary immigrant in the streets with all sorts of fanciful schemes is not to be trusted. Only disinterested persons should be listened to – if they can be found. Care must be taken even with government emigrant agents and members of the emigrant societies, who are there to protect the immigrant from impostors, for they, too, have interests of their own that might be at variance with those of the newcomer. The agents and society members are often intent on developing their own part of the country through encouraging settlement at the expense of other areas. They might also be heavily involved with large land-holders or, indeed, may hold land themselves. Nor should the immigrant relax his vigilance once he is aboard the steamboats on his way into the interior. His trunks should be roped as well as locked and kept under surveillance at all times. Some immigrants have found it necessary to take shifts in watching over one another's baggage with loaded guns. Even then, articles have been stolen.

Emigration societies on the other side of the Atlantic, such as the three in Glasgow, wisely provide the means of support for a period after landing in the colony, so that the migrants will be "relieved from the temptations that too often beset emigrants of the poorer class before their arrival at their final destination." In the spring of 1841 the Glasgow societies also collected no fewer than 3500 articles of clothing for the use of emigrants as well as provisions for the voyage. Among those assisted was a group of 180 men, women, and children, mostly hand-loom weavers, a small portion of the many thousands who have seen their crafts being replaced by the noisy machines of the new industrial age.

It is always difficult for the tired and exhausted settlers to grasp the vast distances they are forced to travel in reaching their destinations. All is a blur of crowded steamers, cramped bateaux, clattering coaches, crude wagons, and sore feet. There are nights in smoky inns, jammed with boisterous drinkers oblivious of the whimpering of the immigrant children. It is as if no one yet realizes how valuable these children are; in the bush they will soon become sources of wealth and no longer the burdens they had been back in the old country.

A great deal of the drinkers' chatter usually concerns the land the settler hopes to get, and how good land can be told from bad when all is in forest. Some people argue that the kind of soil can be determined easily by simply observing the types of trees it supports. For most sorts of agriculture, it is said that a mixture of hard and soft wood trees without too much underbrush should be looked for. Cedar indicates swamps; pine, poor sandy soil; but a mixture of ash, beech, birch, walnut, and maple means the best land. Yet there are others who regard all this as nonsense: land can not be judged by the timber growing on it, they counter, and then they offer proof with examples of land rich in maples that is not worth clearing and of pine forests underlain by fine clay soils.

With the exception of pines, Canadian trees run their shallow roots along the ground. Once clearing is begun, exposed trees are liable to be blown down. That is why newly cut roads on windy days can be even more hazardous than usual for travel. That is also why no shade trees are left in the clearings to shelter the cabin from the scorching summer sun. In time, when a permanent dwelling is built, trees might be planted nearby in an attempt to reproduce the landscape left behind in the old country. It is considered wise to choose the final site for the house only after much of the land has been cleared. Otherwise, it might be discovered, when it is too late, that better sites existed. A high, airy position is considered best. Good air is essential to good health. Malodorous stumps in a certain state of decay are thought by some people to be injurious, and considerable pain and expense is resorted to in having them dug out, dried, and then burned.

The prudent settler will choose his land with at least as much thought about situation as about the quality of soil. Access to good water carriage is essential. Without it, even the best land is of little value since the farmer will be unable to get his wheat or other produce to market. (Roads are generally so poor they are hardly worth considering.) In Britain with its well-developed system of canals, roads, and, most recently, railways, situation is much less important and soil is almost everything in choosing land. Life in Canada requires many such adjustments in the thinking and habits of the newcomer.

Barns are far more essential in Canada than in many parts of the old country. In fact, they are often the best building on any new farmstead, outshining the family's humble log dwelling. Unlike Britain, animals must be kept indoors during the three or four coldest months. During the first winter or two, cattle and oxen are fed on boughs of spruce and hemlock. This "browse" is already familiar to the animals from having wandered in the woods during the summer. As more land is cleared and planted, there will be hay to pitch into the barn's high loft and winter feed such as turnips, mangel-wurzel, and potatoes for storage in the deep pits dug below the frost line. During the first years of settlement, horses are little used since they require greater care than oxen. Sheep, so important in Britain, are difficult to keep and, because of the wolves, must be carefully penned at night. (In the long-settled parts of the country, wolves are now becoming rare and it is expected that before long they will disappear, just as they did long ago in the old country.)

Two crops, still largely unfamiliar in Great Britain, are important in the Canadian settlements: Indian corn and pumpkin. They are usually grown together in the same field. Indeed, one of the most memorable sights on the pioneer farm is the autumn field of golden corn stalks interspersed with orange pumpkins. British settlers soon acquire a taste for corn-on-the-cob and for pumpkin pies. Corn and pumpkin are also fed to the animals. Cattle like a bit of salt with their raw pumpkin. If they eat it exclusively, their flesh acquires a fine gold colour.

Settlers soon learn to make potash from the burning of felled trees. The ashes are gathered, leached, and the solution reduced in large iron pots – hence the name of the finished product. The potash is mostly exported to Great Britain, where it is used in bleaching, in medicines, in making glass and soap, and for other purposes. Some of the newcomers had been involved in a similar activity a few decades earlier in the Scottish Highlands, when kelp was gathered, dried, and burned between layers of peat to produce another alkali used in the same industries. Today, kelping is largely a memory, the industry having collapsed with the importation of cheaper barilla from Spain. Kelping had been a miserable occupation and the poor Highlanders working in it were said to be much worse off than black slaves in the American south. Without even the meager earnings from burning kelp to sustain them, many of these workers ended up in Canada.

Potash making in Canada is also an unpleasant task, but it was often the first "cash crop" in newly settled areas. However, recent advances in chemistry and the use of soda and other substitutes have greatly reduced the price paid for potash in Great Britain. Unless the settler is well situated near cheap transport, potash is now hardly worth the trouble of making it. In the long run it is probably better simply to collect the ashes and use them as fertilizer.

The unsightly appearance of the stump-filled clearings can be quite offensive to the eye of the new settler, still holding memories of the open and level fields of his homeland. Yet it will not be long

"Chatham is emphatically a new town, having been known as such, only about eight or ten years. Within a stone's throw of the principal street, are yet to be seen the relics of the stately forest trees, whose giant tops oft' bowed to the passing breeze, and whose roots still cling to mother earth ... But they, like everything else, will soon disappear and be forgotten."

Western Herald, Sandwich (Windsor), 30 June 1841

6th Street, Chatham, Upper Canada, 1838, by P.J. Bainbrigge. Watercolour, NAC

BIRTH OF A TOWN

"The erection of a saw mill is always the first marked event in the formation of a settlement in the Bush. At first, some one or two adventurers, possessed of a little capital, purchase a few acres of land on the bank of a river or stream, where, in the provincial idiom, there is good water power; two or three rude huts or shanties are erected, and a small clearing is made in the forest; by degrees, others are attracted to the spot: the original settler, meanwhile, has turned a little money, and embarks in a saw mill; this induces many to come into the neighbourhood, from the facility it offers for building. Then, as the settlement increases, some bold man is persuaded to erect a grist or flour mill, which again serves as an attraction; a growing population requires the necessaries of life at hand; stores are opened, a tavern licensed, and in a few years a thriving village, or as in the case of Peterboro', an important town, springs up in the heart of the forest."

Thomas Need, *Six Years in the Bush, 106–7*

before he adjusts to this new normality of life. In a few years the stumps will be gone. Meanwhile, they will do little to hinder the growth of the wheat and other crops planted among them.

A stand of maple is often spared for the making of sugar. As with the preparation of potash, sugar making is a laborious task but, unlike potash, one that is looked forward to eagerly each spring. The new settler soon learns how to tap the maple trees and to collect the sap in homemade wooden troughs. These troughs are emptied into buckets and carried to the steaming sugar kettles, boiling fiercely over an open fire. There are usually at least two kettles – one to boil the sap down to syrup and another to reduce the syrup to sugar. There is a picnic-like atmosphere in the sugar shed as all members of the family enjoy the heat of the fire, the smell of the boiling syrup, and the reward of the finished sugar. Since six gallons of sap is needed to make one pound of sugar, a great deal of work is required not only in collecting the sap but also in cutting and preparing the wood for the fires. There is something very touching about the little sugar cabins, silent in the snowy woods of December 1841; the neatly piled wood under the eaves and the waiting iron kettles are statements of faith that life will return to the land. On the making of sugar, one emigrants' guide has suggested that "the labour is severe but the reward is sweet." In truth, the same could be said about the whole process of settling in the bush.

Chapter Three

The Annihilation of Space and Time

Ian Alexander Bell Robertson was familiar with the phrase "the annihilation of space and time" before he saw it in the *Montreal Transcript* in the summer of 1841. Indeed, it was a favourite of Lord Cockburn, one of his walking companions on The Meadows in Edinburgh. Cockburn predicted that by the mid-1850s, railways were likely to bring London to within fifteen hours of Edinburgh. This might bring about increased wealth and ease, he said, but it would also allow London to predominate at the expense of native talent, manners, amusements, habits, and institutions in smaller cities such as Edinburgh. Separate provincial characters would be lost in the general mass, just as the picturesque peculiarities of the old personal characters of the individual were already being melted in the fusion of common society.

Cockburn and Robertson had both seen phenomenal changes in travel and transport during their lifetimes. They were born in the age of the stagecoach, came to maturity during a phase of rapid canal building, and had lived to see a network of steam railways spreading across the British countryside. By the time Robertson returned to Scotland in 1842, the Edinburgh and Glasgow Railway had opened to the public, an event that had not pleased Lord Cockburn since the line ran through the public garden between the Castle and Princes Street, resulting in "pollution," to use his word. Meanwhile, both men witnessed the advent of steamboats on the Forth and in 1840 Robertson sailed to Halifax on one of the first crossings of the steamer *Britannia*. He completed the journey to Quebec on another Cunard steamer, the *Unicorn*. In 1842 he returned to Great Britain on the *Acadia*. Before leaving Canada, he saw one of the first ships employing the Ericsson screw propeller.

Robertson was acutely aware that changing modes of transport and communication were altering the traveller's perception of the countryside and that information and ideas were being transmitted ever more rapidly. Like Cockburn, he was not convinced that all of these changes were necessarily for the good.

Nowhere is the feeling of optimism more apparent than in the field of transportation. It seems that at last the St Lawrence canals will be completed, and that construction may soon begin on several projected railways. As 1841 draws to a close, there is a great deal of excitement surrounding the introduction of the first screw propellers.

The appearance of the propeller in Canada, just four years after its first application in an experimental boat launched on the Thames, is only the latest example of how quickly Canada has taken up (and often improved upon) new technology in the field of transportation. From the beginning of the country, fur traders made use of the Algonkian Indian canoe, enlarging and adapting it to fit the needs of the trade. Early Canadians also adopted the Indian snowshoe and toboggan. Nothing from Europe was as useful in the soft, deep snows of the Canadas.

Steam navigation came to Canada in November 1809, when John Molson's *Accommodation* made her maiden run from Montreal down to Quebec – just two years after Robert Fulton's *Clermont* went into service between New York and Albany on the Hudson. For the awaiting crowd the *Accommodation*'s arrival must have been a truly novel occurrence. There before them was a craft powered by neither wind nor muscle but by machinery. New sounds and sights were experienced for the first time: the thunderous roar of escaping steam; the heartbeat of the engine as the boat eerily took on a life of its own; the gentle slapping of the paddles on the water; the shower of red sparks from the black funnel; and the dark trail of softwood smoke drifting above the river. In a very few years all of this would become commonplace. Today, in 1841, it is hard to believe that there are still many people under the age of fifty who can remember when there were only sails on the river.

The *Accommodation* was not a financial success. Its Canadian-built machinery had not been sufficiently strong for the current, even after a lot of tinkering to improve it. (Fulton had obtained his machinery from the famous British firm of Boulton and Watt.) However, Molson was far from discouraged and two years later he replaced the *Accommodation* with the first of a long line of successful steamers which he and his family would operate on the St Lawrence. Unlike Fulton, who had been granted a twenty-year monopoly by the United States Congress (upset by the Supreme Court in 1820) for steam navigation in New York State, Molson had been unable to secure exclusive rights in Canada. Even so, the St Lawrence belonged to him until 1815, the year he was first challenged by John Torrance. From then onward, the Molsons and Torrances have dominated the river but they have never been able to make it completely their own.

In the days of sail, a trip from Quebec to Montreal and back was a labour of some weeks. With the advent of the *Accommodation,* the easier downward journey could be accomplished in just sixty-six hours. Year by year this time was reduced until, today, the steamers regularly make the trip in only twelve to fourteen hours in either direction. The first engines had not been powerful enough to allow the steamers to escape the bonds of wind and tide completely. At Quebec, departures were timed for low water in order to pass at full flood through the Richelieu Rapids, about fifty miles further up river. Below Montreal, teams of oxen or horses were kept on hand to provide assistance in going up the St Mary's Rapids. Within a few years, however, stronger engines were generally in use and the last vestiges of nature's imposed rhythms gave way to the measured time of man. Canada's two largest cities, Quebec and Montreal, became neighbours, and everywhere in the Canadas the feeling of isolation is being swiftly dissipated as more and more steamers penetrate into formerly remote corners of the country.

Never before has man experienced such rapid change as that which has taken place during the past thirty years in Canada, Great Britain, the United States, and in a few countries in Western Europe. Whether he realizes it or not, the Canadian's perception of the world is being altered radically. "Now-a-days Steam has in one sense almost annihilated both space and time," said the *Montreal Transcript* in August 1841, "all the world is set in motion; and if such improvements continue to progress for thirty years more, it is impossible to foresee the changes which will take place in the social habits as well as in the individual characters of men." Whether these changes are entirely for the good, the *Transcript* is not at all certain: there is reason to fear that ease of movement is leading to "an unsteadiness of disposition and aversion to regular industry" on the part of the populace; but there is also reason to hope "that much of that narrow spirit of prejudice which tends to keep communities and nations at variance and to breed wars, will disappear, in proportion as freer intercourse banishes the ignorance which generally lies at the root of intolerance and prejudice."

Certainly, friends and relatives can now visit one another more frequently than in the past, and new acquaintances can be made on board the steamers themselves. Sporting teams and individual sportsmen who were formerly restricted to their home areas now can be seen travelling to distant places to challenge their rivals. Perhaps none is more conspicuous than a hunting gentlemen at Quebec who travels with his horse. Man and horse can be observed at the Quebec steamer wharf boarding the evening boat. By breakfast time they are in Trois-Rivières, where they are joined by the man's father-in-law, who keeps a pack of foxhounds. After a good morning of hunting, man and beast can be seen taking the afternoon boat back to Quebec.

In summer, steam draws many tourists to Canada. Europeans are lured by the "sublime grandeur"; Americans, especially those from the deep south, are drawn by the cooler summer temperatures. Niagara Falls or Quebec are the usual starting points, with stops at Toronto, Kingston, and Montreal en route. Few visitors stray far from the waterways. That is why the "views" they leave us almost inevitably show water in the foreground. Because they travel quickly, their perceptions of the Canadas are quite different from those of visitors only a few decades ago.

That perceptions of the countryside are dependent on the mode of travel was commented on by Dr Oliver Goldsmith even before the advent of steam: he noted that a man on foot would necessarily make very different reflections on the scenes through which he passed than would a man who was whirled along in a carriage. One former resident of Canada, Edwin Talbot, who had travelled not by stage-coach but in vehicles which carried him "over the lakes and rivers with greater velocity, perhaps, than ever the Doctor saw others whirled along the roads," resolved in the spring of 1820 to undertake a pedestrian tour from the Talbot Settlement in Upper Canada down to Montreal so he might see the country from another point of view. Talbot was exceptional in travelling more slowly and simply than was necessary: most people today choose the most rapid and comfortable means they can afford, and do not hesitate to reject services as being outmoded which only a few years ago they might have praised as being extraordinarily advanced. When speed and comfort are concerned, Canadians seem never to look back.

To hold on to their patrons, proprietors have been forced not only to provide faster and larger boats but have felt obliged to add "improvements." For example, Captain Tate, whose *Lord Sydenham* is said to be exceeded by none in accommodation, nevertheless felt compelled to add a band during the spring of this year. One traveller, not yet jaded by this latest innovation, reported that the evening of his departure from Montreal "was more like a Musical Soiree in a private dwelling than a passage on board a steam packet."

THE LORD SYDENHAM

The designers of the *Lord Sydenham* – one of the newest
and probably the finest of the steamers on the St Lawrence
– were able to draw upon the experience of three decades
of steam navigation on the river: her machinery was powerful enough to enable her to ascend the Richelieu and St
Mary's rapids with ease or to tow several vessels up river at
the same time; and her draught was shallow enough to
allow her to navigate in certain sections of the river that
could become very shoal, particularly in late summer. The
shallow draught necessitated a broad design which gave
the ship a compact appearance, especially when compared
with the long, narrow transatlantic steamers. Such a
design, of course, would not have been suitable for the
open ocean or, for that matter, even the Great Lakes.
Indeed, she was quite unstable, particularly when loaded
with passengers, animals, and freight. Should she get into
trouble, however, her shallow draught would allow her to
be run into shore. This was just as well since she carried
only one small quarter boat and her crew was poorly
trained for dealing with emergencies. Like other steamers,
the *Lord Sydenham* was frequently overloaded, especially
during times when the immigrants were swarming into
Quebec: hordes of them were swept onto competing steamboats as soon as their ships put into port and it was not
uncommon for a boat to depart for Montreal with up to a
thousand passengers crowding her decks. The *Lord Sydenham* could complete the trip from Quebec to Montreal in
as little as twelve hours and fifteen minutes running time,
not counting stops which could add another two hours or
so. Who could have predicted, three decades earlier, that
the day would come when travel time between Quebec and
Montreal would no longer be measured in days but in
hours – and even in minutes?

The gentility of a soirée is not the usual ambience of the fast life on the steamers. Drunken scenes are common and the newspapers wax lugubriously in their accounts of "melancholy incidents" of travellers falling overboard or slipping from gang-planks while hurrying to catch a departing ship after a few too many at a dockside tavern. (Such incidents are also a normal part of the day-excursions that are popular during the heat of summer.) Departures and landings on dark, stormy nights are especially hazardous to the lives of passengers as they pick their way along the slippery, often rotten, planks of low-lying wharves, frequently with the waves lapping their feet.

FALLING OVERBOARD

It was very easy to fall overboard from the steamers as was discovered by a young man, appropriately enough, at Bath on the Bay of Quinte. Finding he could make no headway against the shrill voice of his lady during a lover's quarrel on board the *Sir James Kempt*, he dramatically bid adieu forever and then took a quick step backward and nearly fulfilled his doughty bravado as he plunged over the side into the cold lake below. The night was dark and had it not been for the presence of the men who were loading the boat, he might well have drowned. However, this story had a happy ending for as he was dragged dripping on board, his lady ran to comfort her victim in penitence for having driven him to this dreadful act.

Steam has greatly assisted immigrants in reaching their land grants in time to get settled in during the first season. It has also enabled the produce of their labour to be readily moved from one part of the country to another or to be exported overseas. The local markets in the towns and cities are no longer dependent on their immediate surroundings for produce and they can offer food from greater distances, in larger quantities and at lower prices. This has resulted in an increase in consumption and this increase, in turn, has largely compensated the farmers living near the cities for the declining advantage of their location. Crops can now be concentrated where they do best; for instance, grapes, melons, apples, and pears, which do not do well at Quebec, are now imported from Montreal, where the summers are longer and warmer.

The "annihilation of space and time" has played a role in the increasing number and severity of epidemics. The worst of these were the cholera epidemics of 1832 and 1834. Both began on the lower St Lawrence with the arrival of immigrants from Great Britain and then spread into the interior along the waterways. Only areas which could not be reached by steamer – such as the Eastern Townships of Lower Canada – escaped the fury of the disease. Troops transferred from distant points in the empire are probably another source of exotic diseases. To give but one example: in the summer of 1841 the converted royal yacht *Appolo* (under steam tow) put into Quebec after sailing directly from Jamaica. It would have been most unusual had there been no cases of illness on board.

The steam railway has already allowed London to extend its influence over the whole England. Now the steamship is beginning to strengthen its dominance throughout the empire. Readers of Canadian newspapers are daily exposed to information and ideas from the mother country as well as news about sister colonies and other countries overseas. This comes in the form of items copied from a variety of British newspapers – newspapers that are rushed to Liverpool or Portsmouth by steam railway to catch the last-minute departure of one of the steamships bound for the new world. The ships' arrival in North America always precipitates an unseemly scramble among competing newspaper proprietors. Each is eager to beat his opponent in publishing the first extracts from the British press. The items are usually prefaced with headings such as "nine days later" or "seven days later" indicating news nine days or seven days more recent than the last extracts published. The speed and regularity with which the British newspapers are received has improved noticeably since July 1840, thanks to the introduction of the first regularly scheduled steam mail service between England, British North America, and the United States by Samuel Cunard's British and North American Royal Mail Steam Packet Company.

Cunard's steam packets provide a twice-monthly service between Liverpool and Boston, with a stopover in each direction at Cunard's home town port, Halifax. From Halifax, newspapers and mail destined for the Canadas are usually rushed across the peninsula of Nova Scotia in seventeen hours to Pictou, on the Northumberland Strait, in two double carriages known as the English Mail Cars. There they are quickly transferred to another Cunarder, the *Unicorn*, all steamed up and ready for the journey to Quebec. (Occasionally the *Unicorn* sails directly to Quebec from Halifax, but this means a longer transit for the newspapers and mail.) The mail cars do not carry passengers.

Travellers from the Cunarders bound for the Canadas are forced to hire their own horses and carriages, and gallop into the darkness in pursuit of the mail cars as they speed through the night.

Once on board the *Unicorn*, passengers can begin to relax as they steam past the low, red cliffs of the eastern end of Prince Edward Island. Before long, the land fades into the distance and they are in the Gulf of St Lawrence and on their way to Quebec, the terminus of the steam packet service. It is a tedious trip: seventeen hours in a bouncing coach followed by many more in the nauseating swell of the shallow gulf. Not surprisingly, some Canada-bound passengers prefer to remain on board the Atlantic steamer until Boston and to make their way to Canada from there. It is probably easier to reach Montreal by this round-about route than via Quebec. And faster, too, to judge from the complaints of Canadian newspaper proprietors in the summer of 1841 who were grumbling that newspapers from England were reaching Montreal a day earlier by way of Boston. Whining about the mails being a day or even a few hours late illustrates how each improvement brings with it rising expectations: only a year or two ago the present service would have seemed miraculous; now there is disappointment if the *Unicorn* does not round the cape at Quebec almost to the hour.

Newspapers, mail, and passengers make the twelve- to fourteen-hour trip from Quebec to Montreal on the *Lord Sydenham*, the *Lady Colbourne*, or one of the other Royal Mail steamers. Mail and passengers for destinations above Montreal are carried by the Upper Canada Stage and Steamboat Company as far as Dickenson's Landing. As its name implies, the company uses both water and land transport. This is necessitated by the rapids on the upper St Lawrence. At Dickenson's Landing the coach links up with a waiting steamer, either the *Gildersleeve* or the *Brockville*, which sails for Kingston on alternate days. Stops along the way are made at Gananoque, Brockville, Maitland, Prescott, Ogdensburg, Matilda, and Williamsburg. At Kingston one of the overnight lake steamers bound for Toronto – the *St George*, the *Niagara*, or the *City of Toronto* – awaits the arrival of the newspapers, mail, and passengers. On the way to Toronto stops are made at Cobourg and Port Hope. Mail and passengers, of course, are taken on and put off all along the way.

The downward mail and passenger service from Toronto to Montreal, Quebec, and Halifax is similar to the service upward. It has now reached such a level of reliability that a correspondent or passenger wishing to take advantage of a specific sailing from Halifax can easily calculate the latest time a letter should be posted, or a ship boarded, at various places along the route, even in the distant interior. For example, letters reach Quebec in four or five days from

CUNARD STEAMERS

Samuel Cunard's success in securing the British mail contract was remarkable considering that he alone of the three bidders had no ships to offer. In fact, all he had to show at the time were plans for three vessels of similar design, built to assure regularity of service. His contenders had ships of differing sizes and speeds, making it difficult to provide regularly scheduled crossings. Among these ships were the *Great Western*, designed by Brunel and owned by the Great Western Company, and the *British Queen* and the *President*, which belonged to the British and American Steam Navigation Company. Launched in 1838 and 1839, respectively, the *British Queen* and the *President* were considerably larger, roomier, and more comfortable than the *Great Western*, their slightly older rival, but, unfortunately, they lacked its reserve power and strong hull.

The first three Cunarders, the *Britannia*, the *Acadia*, and the *Caledonia*, began service in 1840. A fourth, the *Columbia*, was added in 1841. The Cunarders were designed for carrying nothing but fuel, mail, passengers, and luggage. Narrow and light, they had more in common with Brunel's *Great Western* than with the luxurious *British Queen* and *President*. They were the fastest ships on the Atlantic, but they tended to roll excessively in heavy seas.

About six months after Cunard's ships went into service, the public was treated to a "race" between the *Britannia* and the *British Queen*. Both ships sailed at one o'clock on 1 December, the *Britannia* from Boston for Liverpool and the *British Queen* from New York for Portsmouth. The distances were nearly equal: the *Britannia* nosed into Liverpool on the evening of the 14th, just thirteen and a half days out of Boston and eleven and a half from Halifax; the *British Queen* did not reach Portsmouth for another week, after a passage of twenty and a half days. From Portsmouth the *British Queen* continued on to London, her final destination. Such comparisons of performance greatly damaged the reputations of the New York steamers. Only a year or two earlier their speeds were considered wonderfully swift, but hardly had the Cunarders appeared on the scene before these times were seen as inadequate in an age of ever increasing speed. The number of passengers began to fall off and it soon became obvious that the liners would fail. Then, in March 1841, the top-heavy *President* disappeared during a westbound sailing. For months afterwards the huge three-decker ship was reported sighted in various parts of the Atlantic but as the summer went on it became increasingly apparent that she had gone beneath the waves forever. The loss of the *President* was a fatal blow to the ailing British and American Steam Navigation Company and in August it sold the *British Queen* to the Belgian government. By the end of the year, the *Great Western* was also up for sale.

Cunard's ships were cramped and they rolled badly, but they were successful because Cunard correctly judged the public mind by offering speed at the expense of comfort. And his ships *were* fast: in July 1841 the *Britannia* steamed from Boston to Liverpool in just twelve days, and in only nine days and twenty hours from Halifax which, according to her jocose commander, was the fastest crossing "since the Atlantic was the Atlantic." As in all Atlantic steamer crossings at that time, the ship was propelled both by her sails and her machinery. With such successes behind them, it was not surprising to learn that late in 1841 the Cunard interests were negotiating with the government to accelerate their service further by increasing the frequency of sailings from twice monthly to once weekly.

Britannia.
Frontispiece,
Charles Dickens,
American
Notes
and Pictures
from Italy
(London:
Macmillan 1893)

Faster ships and the mail contract, which amounted to a government subsidy, were not the only advantages Cunard's line had over its rivals: its Liverpool-Halifax-Boston route was superior to that of its New York competitors – not only was it shorter but, with the Halifax coaling stopover, considerably less space was required for fuel than was necessary on the New York ships that went directly to England. This, of course, meant more room on the Cunarders for mail, passengers, and baggage. Moreover, boats which were not fully loaded with fuel operated more efficiently because they did not sit as low in the water and thus their paddles could perform more effectively. As the coal was burned during the crossing, ships would rise ever higher in the water; that is why they often ended their journeys at speeds considerably faster than when they set out. Each Cunarder carried 115 passengers. None of them was steerage, which, according to Captain Barclay of Ury, the gentleman farmer from Scotland who crossed on the *Britannia* in April 1841, made "the company select"; accordingly, he had never "before met as numerous a company, strangers to each other, so agreeable and anxious to make things mutually pleasant." Nine months later, the twenty-nine-year-old Charles Dickens braved a winter crossing on the *Britannia*; his amusing account of life on board the rolling ship can be found in his *American Notes*.

Hamilton or Niagara, and in three or four days from Toronto, depending upon whether a Sunday intervenes or not. Another five days are required for letters to reach Halifax from Quebec. Thus a letter for the departure of Cunard's *Britannia* from Halifax on 19 July 1841, if entered at the post office at Toronto by 9 July, would have reached Liverpool at 7 PM on the 29th – just twenty days from Toronto. Such rapid communication has done much to reduce the distance separating the immigrant from his loved ones back in the old country. This is especially true during the open season from May to October. During the winter, the post can still be quite slow and correspondents were advised by the *Quebec Mercury* "to regulate their periods for writing home accordingly."

The prepaid penny-post reform introduced in Great Britain in 1840 does not yet apply to the colonies, where postage charges are still high – the equivalent of two or three days of a labourer's wages – and are still paid by the recipient. No tantalization can be more terrible than that faced by the poor immigrant who presents himself at the post office to claim a letter from home, only to be turned away because he lacks the money to pay for it. What is in the letter? Is a friend or relative from his village coming to settle near him in the bush? Has his ailing mother died? Has his plain little sister found a man? Not surprisingly, many settlers rely on newly arrived immigrants to bring them letters from friends and relatives in the old country. Few of these letters bear recent dates. Like the immigrants who carry them to the cabin in the bush, the letters have taken weeks to cross the Atlantic on a slow sailing ship: few migrants can afford to cross by steamer. For the poor, Great Britain remains far away; perhaps it is not surprising that ties with the old country are soon broken and that in a generation or two all knowledge of where they had come from will be lost to the settler's descendants. Yet on a more abstract level, the man in the bush (like his fellow colonist in the town) is aware of the British news that is trickling in through the newspapers. As a result, he seems to be taking an increased pride in being part of a great and growing empire. Indeed, the *Montreal Transcript* feels that it is no longer a figure of speech to talk of the *public mind* of empire. In Halifax, where it is possible to read London newspapers only twelve days late or Liverpool papers even a day sooner, the *Novascotian* claimed it was possible to imagine oneself on the Plains of Mayo or in the Highlands of Scotland.

In the larger centres there are reading rooms where newspapers are available from Canada and abroad. These are popular gathering places for merchants, mechanics (tradesmen), and others who wish to keep up with the outside world. Newspapers are also to be found in the taverns, where they are often read aloud and discussed. In

STEAMER CITY OF TORONTO

Built by the Niagara Dock Company, the *City of Toronto* was said to be "as splendid a specimen of naval architecture as almost any country can exhibit." Unlike most lake steamers, her hull design permitted her to be ship rigged. In this she was more like Cunard's *Acadia*, after which she was modelled. The addition of sails not only improved her speed but greatly reduced the amount of fuel required by her two powerful engines. They could generate over one hundred horsepower and added greatly to the vessel's safety during storms. Portions of the engines as well as the startling figurehead came from the Clyde, birthplace of the *Acadia*. The figurehead, carved by an eminent artist, depicted an Indian chief who stood six feet three in his moccasins and, with a tomahawk in one hand and a knife in the other, looked furious enough to frighten an army of "pale faces."

The sails and the comparatively deep draft of the *City of Toronto* illustrated the main difference between navigation on the Great Lakes and on the St Lawrence: on the relatively narrow river with its winding channel and shoals, sails were much less useful, especially during the difficult upward journey when the prevailing westerlies offered little assistance against the current; but on the ocean-like lakes, where currents were no problem, sails could be used in much the way they were on the high seas. Sailing ships would probably continue to be operated on the Great Lakes, side by side with the steamers, particularly for moving cargoes destined for points along the lake front where time was not important. Along the St Lawrence, however, Sir Richard Bonnycastle was predicting as early as 1841 that "the day is not far distant when no sailing vessel will be seen on this mighty stream."

The
Princess Royal,
sister ship to the
City of Toronto.
Metropolitan
Toronto
Reference Library,
J. Ross Robertson
Collection,
2563

Lower Canada the barrier of language restricts most French Canadians to their own local papers. Out in the countryside, where literacy is not high, news from the outside is relayed through the parish priest or other educated persons. Local gossip is exchanged amidst the sighs and laughter of the knots of people gathered at the church door after mass. Unlike many of his newly arrived English-speaking compatriots, the French Canadian's ties with the old world have long since been broken. He is firmly rooted in the soil of Canada and thinks of himself not as a French Canadian but, simply, as a Canadian.

For the most part, French Canadians occupy only the humbler positions in the transportation industry within Canada. Even in Lower Canada, where they might make up most of the crew on a St Law-

> Steam also made possible the rapid communication of scientific information and ideas. In the summer of 1841 Sir Charles Lyell, the great Victorian geologist, was able to spend a Saturday in Halifax only eleven days after leaving Liverpool on the *Acadia*; he visited the city and its museum, where he studied a fossil tree; then he wrote letters home, which were put on board the Liverpool-bound *Caledonia* the next day. Within a month of his departure from Great Britain, his letters with news about the new world were in the hands of his friends in the old country – thanks to the Atlantic steam packets and the growing network of railways in England.

rence steamer, they seldom become officers or captains. However, they do operate many of the smaller boats, such as the bateaux on the upper St Lawrence and the ferries and ice-boats between Quebec and Lévis. Most of the steamships are owned by English-speaking merchants and forwarders, and it is they who are most keenly interested in improving navigation on the St Lawrence and the Great Lakes.

Many more lighthouses are needed along the St Lawrence-Great Lakes route. Even on the broad river below Montreal, travel is very dangerous with inexperienced seamen, especially during dark nights or hazy weather – a danger that is greatly increased by a channel which shifts from year to year and by the presence of many shoals. The latter were unusually troublesome during the dry summer of 1841, when the river had "scarcely ever been known to be so shallow."

Near Montreal, late in October, the
steamer *Princess Victoria* had her bottom staved in when she struck a rock
while making one of her regular crossings to La Prairie, where she connects
with the railway for St John's. Below
the city, the most dangerous portion
of the St Lawrence is probably in a wide,
shallow section known as Lake St Peter. Even at the best of times the "lake"
is quite shallow and it is the cause of
some vessels bound for overseas being

forced to leave Montreal with only partial loads. These vessels are
usually topped off at Quebec before heading for the high seas.

Light-tower, near Coburg by W.H. Bartlett. In Willis, Canadian Scenery, vol. 2, facing p. 55

Above Montreal the river is also more dangerous than usual, especially at the Long Sault and Cedar rapids where navigation is per-
ilous even in a good year. During a ten-day period in October and
early November, twelve barges laden with produce from Kingston
met with accidents at the rapids; all cargoes, mostly wheat and flour,
were damaged to a greater or lesser extent. Unloading the water-
soaked wheat and the barrels of paste was a very discouraging task,
but there is reason to hope that such work will soon be a thing of
the past: the British loan guarantee for finishing the canals, along
with the Ericsson screw propeller, in use since June, both give promise
of safer navigation in the immediate future. It seems that soon ships
that are safe on the ocean-like Great Lakes will be able to make the
trip down to Montreal. No longer will goods passing through the
upper St Lawrence need to be transshipped on bateaux, Durham

Left: Durham boat; Right: bateau, by W.H. Bartlett. In Willis, Canadian Scenery, vol. 2, facing p. 46

boats, or barges similar to the ones that carried the damaged wheat and flour. The completion of the canals will allow the largest steamers now sailing the lakes to carry goods directly to Montreal, where they can be transferred to ships destined for overseas ports. This will take time. For now, the Ericsson screw propeller seems to offer the best possibility for securing a safe means for sending goods down to Montreal.

The first boats in Canada employing the Ericsson screw are probably the four small, decked barges built at Brockville for Messrs Murray and Sanderson. Three are using machinery from New York but one has "an ingenious engine and propeller" built by Nelson Walker of Montreal from only "a mere theoretic sketch of Ericsson's invention." Although small for steamers – they carry only 110 tons or 1000 barrels of flour – their narrow beam and absence of side-paddles mean they can pass through the locks of the existing canals. Since going into service in June, the little "propellers," as the boats are known, have proved their worth in the role for which they were designed: the circumnavigation of the Kingston-Montreal-Bytown-Kingston "island." Going down to Montreal they follow the St Lawrence; returning, they travel by way of the Ottawa and the Rideau Canal; the full circuit takes five or six days if there are no delays at the locks. With screw propulsion not only are the little craft largely independent of wind and weather but, unlike sailboats and broad-beamed paddle-boats, they can descend the rapids without having to wait for a fair wind.

Although the first Ericsson steamers are considered a success, they are too small to be operated safely on the Great Lakes. This has prompted merchants to call for a vessel that can navigate the lakes, shoot the rapids of the St Lawrence, and still get through the narrow locks. In November, just such a vessel appeared on the scene – the *Vandalia*. She can carry 140 tons and, at twenty feet two inches wide and ninety feet long, she is designed to squeeze through the locks of the Welland Canal, which connects Lake Ontario and Lake Erie. To save fuel on the lakes, she is sloop rigged.

By the end of 1841 the *Kingston Chronicle and Gazette* was optimistically predicting a whole new era in steam navigation: no longer would there be any necessity for remaining in idleness, cooped up in harbour for days or weeks waiting for a wind. The farmer or the merchant at Goderich in the far western end of the province would soon ship his wheat, flour, pork, and ashes on a Monday morning confident that they would arrive in Montreal as soon as his letter of advice reached his merchant there. Since no transshipment would be necessary, the risk involved would be diminished by half, as would the cost of freight. On the return trip, the vessels would leave Montreal with 100 tons of dry goods and salt bound for one or more of the ports on Lakes Erie, St Clair, or Huron, making the upward journey in just ten days. The cost of both imports and exports would thus be reduced, "adding to the riches of the farmer, extending the business of the merchants and increasing the wealth of the province." In other words, the *Vandalia* was promising, if only on a limited scale, many of the economic advantages that would accrue from the improvements projected for the St Lawrence-Great Lakes waterway.

Uncompleted Cornwall Canal at the Long Sault. **Long Sault Rapid on the St. Laurence** *by W.H. Bartlett. In Willis,* **Canadian Scenery,** *vol. 1, facing p. 46*

The St Lawrence canals, with their 45 foot by 180 foot locks, are designed to accommodate lake vessels and accordingly are much larger and more costly to build than other canals, which are generally intended only for barges and, possibly, schooners. Even in its uncompleted state, the Long Sault section of the eleven-mile Cornwall Canal exemplifies the enormous effort and accomplishment to date. It is an impressive achievement, especially when the climate, the remoteness, and the small population of the Canadas are considered. The massive works were begun in 1834, but later had to be abandoned when the contractors ran into financial difficulties because of the sudden and unprecedented rise in the cost of provisions and labour in 1835 and 1836. Since then the partially completed canal has been deteriorating rapidly in the harsh Canadian climate. Each month of delay is adding to the final cost.

Completion of the Cornwall Canal will permit steamboat navigation from the head of Lake Ontario to Coteau-du-Lac at the lower end of Lake St Francis. At Coteau-du-Lac and again at the Cedars and the Cascades (both in Lower Canada) there are difficult rapids

ERICSSON SCREW PROPELLER

Canada has been remarkably open to the acceptance of new technology, especially in the realm of transportation and communication: only four years after the first ship employing the Ericsson engine and screw propeller was launched in England, craft employing similar machinery were being built and used in Canada. Swedish-born John Ericsson had developed his propeller in England but was disappointed when it was rejected by the Lords of the Admiralty. He did, however, receive a great deal of encouragement from the United States consul at Liverpool, Francis B. Ogden, after whom he named his first experimental boat, which was launched on the Thames in 1837. Shortly after its rejection by the Admiralty, the propeller was taken up by Captain Stockton of the United States Navy, who promised Ericsson that "we'll make your name ring on the Delaware, as soon as we get the propeller there." The captain immediately ordered an iron ship, the *Robert F. Stockton*, to be built in Britain and fitted with an Ericsson engine and screw propeller. Launched in July 1838, the *Stockton* reached New York in May 1839; a few months later Ericsson, himself, came to America.

The Ericsson propeller found immediate acceptance in the United States and, by 1841, its use had spread to Canada. In coming by way of the United States, it had taken a common route by which innovations reached Canada.

Although often referred to as the "inventor of the propeller," Ericsson was more accurately described as being one of the more recent, and successful, innovators who had taken up the old and well-known principle of the water-screw. His engine was smaller and lighter than others then in use and, because it was placed lower in the boat and in the stern, it not only freed valuable space for cargo but also acted as ballast; it was also more efficient and so less space was required for carrying fuel. In part, the greater efficiency of his engine was achieved through a more direct application of power to the propellers, which were rotated at greater speed than was possible with paddle wheels. The weight of the big wheels – the larger part of them were above the water line – greatly reduced the carrying capacity of the vessel, whereas the screws, weighing only about one-twentieth as much, were a negligible burden, especially since they were completely submerged beneath the water. Unlike the paddles, whose wash frequently caused damage to the banks of ca-

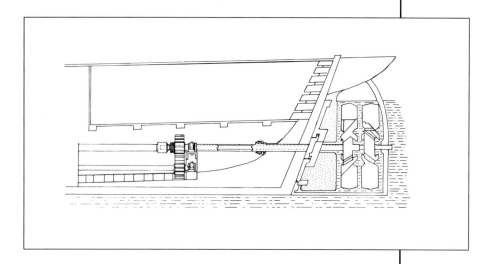

nals and rivers, the action of the screw was said to leave the water relatively undisturbed and hence did little harm; and, being beneath the surface, it was less vulnerable than the paddle to damage by ice, logs, and other floating debris. To accommodate paddles, steamers were usually of a broad design, with the paddles and boxes adding further to the breadth. Such craft could not negotiate the narrower canals or be fitted with sails for use on the open lakes. Ericsson vessels, in contrast, could be designed along the narrow lines of conventional sailing ships and, when there was a good wind, the screw could be disconnected to allow the ship to proceed under canvas at great savings in fuel.

Ericsson's Screw Propellers in the Robt. F. Stockton. 1839. From Benet Woodcroft, A Sketch of the Origin and Progress of Steam Navigation (London 1848), opp. 98. Redrawn by Peter Ennals

that are yet to be overcome. Like those at the Long Sault, these rapids cannot be safely navigated by descending vessels of a large size if heavily laden. It is true that there are locks at the Cedars, but they are too small for boats capable of navigation on the lakes. Further down river near Montreal is the Lachine Canal. Its twenty-foot stone locks also limit its use to small boats. There has been talk of widening the canal, but for a number of reasons – including the necessity of closing the canal while work is in progress – it is now thought to be more practical to make a new canal.

Since the late 1830s, lake steamers have been powerful enough to shoot the rapids of the St Lawrence safely from Lake Ontario down river to Dickenson's Landing – a point just above the Long Sault. Here passengers and goods are exchanged for the poor wretches and battered parcels that have just arrived on one of the regularly scheduled stagecoaches that rattle over the notorious, bone-shattering portage by-passing the rapids. From the banks of the mighty river, steamers descending to Dickenson's Landing seem pathetically small as they pitch and roll down the foaming rapids. On the upward journey, their engines pound defiantly as they inch up the rapids, barely gaining on the dark plumes puffing from the tall thin funnels.

At the western end of Lake Ontario the way to Lake Erie and the upper lakes beyond is blocked by Niagara Falls. To by-pass the falls, the Welland Canal was built a decade or two ago. Its forty locks can accommodate schooners but not steamers. Curiously, the locks vary in size. Since the smallest lock determines the maximum size of vessels that can use the canal, the larger locks are not being used to full advantage. The smaller locks were originally twenty-two feet wide – too narrow for broad-beamed steamers – but now some have settled inwardly to no more than twenty and a half feet. The canal is badly run down. To assure its continued operation, the Province of Canada recently took it over, and by the end of the year, a large number of men were employed in making much needed improvements.

During the late war [of 1812] the rapids along the St Lawrence had proved to be such a serious inconvenience in conveying heavy stores into the interior that, shortly after the peace of 1815, a search was made for a new line of communication between Kingston and the Ottawa River that would not only by-pass the rapids but would do so at a sufficiently safe distance from United States territory as not to be exposed to attack. Little was done on the new route until 1826, when Lt-Col. By, Royal Engineers, was sent out to make a canal by way of the Rideau River. Under his superintendence and

A Birds-eye View of the River Niagara from Lake Erie to Lake Ontario,
from a drawing by W.P. Callington, after an actual survey made in 1837.
Metropolitan Toronto Reference Library,
J. Ross Robertson Collection, 221

at the sole expense of the British government, the canal was completed and open for public use in 1832.

The Rideau Canal was designed to enable schooners to pass between the Great Lakes and the St Lawrence. The schooners (or other small vessels) are towed through the canal by specially constructed steam tugboats. These are long and narrow, with rear paddles. The locks are too small for lake steamers.

About the same time as the construction of the Rideau, canals were also dug along the Ottawa at Grenville, Chûte-à-Blondeau, and Carillon by the Royal Staff Corps. All three were regarded as an integral part of the Rideau Canal system. Yet, for some peculiar reason, they, along with the locks at Vaudreuil and Ste-Anne, were narrower than those of the main canal. In fact, they were similar in size to those on the Lachine Canal. Like the Welland Canal, this meant that the larger locks could not be used to full advantage. Until recently, the locks at Vaudreuil and Ste-Anne were privately owned, allowing the commerce on the Rideau, which had been constructed at enormous public expense, to be monopolized by a private company. In 1841, however, public improvements were in progress at Ste-Anne and the entire system is being opened to the public.

The Rideau is important strategically but commercial interests in the Canadas regard it as a long and tedious detour around the main route to the interior along the St Lawrence. They would be pressing for the completion of the St Lawrence canals even if the Rideau Canal could accommodate lake steamers. They believe the Rideau should continue to handle local traffic and be maintained in its strategic military role. Should another war break out with the United States, there is no reason to believe that the Americans would neglect shutting off the St Lawrence to British shipping as they did during the recent war [of 1812]. In war or in other emergencies, the Rideau would be ready and able to provide an alternate life line to the Great Lakes – if only on a limited scale.

The fact that goods from the Great Lakes destined for Montreal and Great Britain have to be transshipped several times not only causes delay and increases the possibility of damage but, more importantly, adds considerably to their cost. This has handicapped the St Lawrence route in its competition with the Erie Canal for the rapidly growing trade between England and the newly opened western states. The cost of shipping by the Erie Canal is already less than by way of the St Lawrence, and will soon become lower still when the work now in progress for enlarging the canal is completed. The only reason that the St Lawrence has been able to hold on to even a portion of the transit trade between the western states and Great Britain is because of the higher duties imposed on certain types of merchandise imported into the United States and the lower duties in favour of colonial produce entering Great Britain. United States goods shipped by way of Canada enter Britain as if they were colonial, after a fee is paid. Advocates of further improvements to the St Lawrence route stress the importance of deflecting more of the western trade from the Erie Canal. They argue that an increase in the volume of the transit trade would benefit Canada in many ways, not the least of which would be the increase in the amount of canal fees collected; these would not only enable the debts incurred in building the canals to be paid off more quickly but, presumably, would enable the charges for using the canals to be kept lower, to the benefit of everyone from farmer and lumberer to the final buyer in Canada or overseas.

The completion of the canals is expected to have a profound effect on a number of towns and cities, especially Quebec, Montreal, Kingston, and Toronto. Like New York on the Hudson and New Orleans on the Mississippi, Quebeckers consider their city to have been intended by providence to become one of "the grand commercial emporiums of North America." Once ships were sailing from her harbour directly into the Great Lakes, her destiny would be fulfilled and she would "attain in the commerce of Canada the position allotted to her by nature" – a position she has seen eroded over the years, first by Montreal and later by Kingston, Toronto, and New York. Now, with the advent of the Ericsson boats in June 1841, perhaps she will not have to await the completion of the canals to regain her rightful place. By October, plans were already afoot to form a forwarding company between Quebec and the west that would take advantage of the "propellers." The project has received strong support in the city from both the English and French newspapers and it is hoped that it will not be "allowed to fall through, as has been the case with so many others." This was a time for everyone to unite behind the proposal and to allow "no petty divisions, no party feelings, and no jealousies of origins" to interfere with carrying it out. Quebec would now become the sole break-in-bulk point for goods to and from overseas, and would thus profit at the expense of Montreal. Steam technology had allowed ocean-going ships to be towed up to Montreal to receive goods from the interior. Now a further development would permit Quebec to regain her rightful position as the entrepôt of Canada.

Kingston would also suffer since there would no longer be a need for wheat and other produce sent from upcountry by lake schooner or steamer to be landed, placed in storage, and later reloaded on barges designed for the canals and rivers below. For several decades the city has profited handsomely from the transit trade. "By break-

RIDEAU CANAL

The Rideau Canal was very much a creation of its time and place, based as it was on an abundance of largely unpopulated land, excellence in engineering, and the coming of steam. It was quite different from other canals and, indeed, throughout most of its 126 miles, was not really a canal at all but rather a series of rivers, streams, and lakes that had been dammed in such a way that they formed a continuous line of water communication. In many places the forest had been drowned, so that navigation took place through vast and eerie swamps of stagnant water amidst dead and decaying

trees. Only in a country where land was abundant and people scarce could such a spend-thrift use be made of huge tracts of good soil. Yet more than just the submerged land was being lost: wherever flooding occurred, lands neighbouring the stagnant waters were considered dangerous to health and were avoided by the settlers. In areas where the waters had been left in their "natural state," settlement had taken place but in many cases the "settlers" were actually "squatters" on land that had been granted or acquired by absentee speculators. Few settlers could afford to pay the high prices demanded by the speculators. Some of them simply squatted, but most pushed on westward to where land could be had for only a third or a fifth as much; thus the Rideau, in spite of being part of an important route into the interior, was still largely an uninhabited wasteland with little commerce or traffic being generated along its empty shores.

JONES'S FALLS DAM AND LOCKS

By any standards, the Rideau Canal was a magnificent engineering achievement: bold in concept and superbly crafted in every detail. Examples of excellence abounded but perhaps none surpassed the works at Jones's Falls, where a steep waterfall in a ravine necessitated the building of a sixty-foot stone dam – more than twice the height of any other in North America – under the most trying wilderness conditions. To one side of the dam a chain of three locks provided an excellent example of the fine masonry construction found throughout the canal.

Jones's Falls Dam and Locks, Rideau, c. 1838, by P.J. Bainbrigge. Watercolour NAC

THE *COLONEL JOHN BY*, RIDEAU TUGBOAT

Before the coming of steam, a canal created in the manner of the Rideau would have been of little practical value: without the possibility of tow paths, and being in several places unfit for the rowing of boats or propelling them with poles, the canal could not have been used effectively without steamboats. Rafts, barges, and other craft were towed by steamboats like the *Colonel John By*. These were provided by private companies called forwarders which, at times, had not been above coming to an agreement for the purpose of excluding competition and setting prices.

In spite of its enormous cost and fine workmanship, the Rideau did not get the patronage that might have been expected. Upwards, the canal received considerable traffic although some shippers continued having their boats laboriously pulled and poled up the St Lawrence Rapids rather than paying the canal tolls. Downward, many preferred taking their chances with shooting the rapids in order to save on both time and cost. That is why the fees downward were set at half those for the upward journey.

The John By, Rideau tugboat with rear paddle for the narrow locks. Metropolitan Toronto Reference Library, J. Ross Robertson Collection, 2550

ing bulk at Kingston," claims the *Toronto Patriot,* "the forwarders, merchants and others of that favoured spot reap a rich harvest, and the cost of carriage of produce from where it is grown, to market, is increased something like fifty per cent or upwards, and a proportionate reduction in price is laid on the poor farmer." The *Patriot* is no friend of Kingston, so the figure of 50 per cent may be exaggerated. However, there is little doubt that the Kingston merchants have exploited their natural advantage to the fullest and that they will suffer accordingly when this advantage is removed. At the same time, the "good City of Toronto" stands to gain from the introduction of the Ericsson boats. In fact, if the *Patriot* is to be believed, no other part of the British settlements will feel the change more strongly. Certainly Toronto is in a good position to profit from any improvement in navigation: not only is it now the largest city in Upper Canada but it possesses a lively commercial class, a fine harbour, and a situation near some of the most fertile agricultural land in either Canada.

The rapid changes in steam technology have altered the possibilities available to individuals as well as to places. Some jobs are being lost, others are being created. The need for bargemen, traditional sailors, and coachmen has been reduced. Men put out of these jobs might find work on the steamers, or in cutting wood to fuel the ships' boilers. The demand for wood is insatiable. Steamer machinery is not very efficient and huge amounts of fuel are necessary. During a trip between Montreal and Quebec an ordinary steamboat consumes fifty to sixty cords in each direction. Were all the wood taken on at the beginning of the journey, little space would remain for passengers and cargo. Wood has to be taken on frequently and that is the reason for the many stockpiles that can be seen along the St Lawrence and other waterways throughout the Canadas. Maintaining these stockpiles has provided a new livelihood for many woodcutters; each man can prepare about two cords a day and, though his life may appear free-and-easy to those passing on the ships, the work is hard and the wages only a dollar per cord – little more than sufficient to cover his maintenance. In the Thousand Islands area, and probably elsewhere as well, labour is the only cost in the price of the wood, since it is taken from government land by cutters who do not trouble the authorities with the payment of value or rents.

Because of the cooler climate, pine is the most available fuel along the St Lawrence. It gives off a pleasant-smelling, dark smoke that betrays the passage of steamers long after they have gone by. Pine is far less efficient than the wood available along the Great Lakes, where a milder climate provides an abundance of hickory, beech, maple, and other hardwoods. It is said that three cords of pine are required to do the work of one of hardwood. With each vessel consuming about 2000 cords a year, easily accessible wood is becoming scarce and prices are increasing – especially in heavily travelled regions. On the busy Hudson, wood now costs three times as much as it does along the St Lawrence and the day is probably not far off when price will dictate its replacement with coal.

Steam has permitted farmers to grow fresh produce for new and more distant markets, and merchants are now able to extend their enterprises into the distant interior. Shipyards are kept busy by the steady demand for new boats, and foundries are finding new opportunities in the production of steam machinery.

The steam railway also promises new types of work, although in 1841 the only line actually built and in operation is the fourteen-mile Champlain & St Lawrence Railway. So far Canada, unlike the mother country and the United States, has focused its attention on water transportation to the detriment of overland improvements. Even the Champlain & St Lawrence is part of a steamer route. In fact, it is actually a portage on the water route between Montreal and New York. Goods and passengers from Montreal are discharged at the wharf at La Prairie, on the south shore of the St Lawrence, across from the city. They are then loaded onto the train for the forty-minute trip to St John's on the Richelieu River. Here they are transferred to a steamer which carries them up the Richelieu and then south through Lake Champlain to Whitehall. From Whitehall to Saratoga Springs they are forced to take to the road, but from Saratoga Springs down to Troy on the Hudson they ride in relative comfort on a railway that is one year older than the Champlain St Lawrence. From Troy they steam the few miles to Albany before beginning the pleasant and scenic run down the Hudson to New York. The entire journey from Montreal to New York can now be accomplished in just two and a half days.

The Champlain & St Lawrence Railway was officially opened in July 1836, just six years after the opening of the Liverpool and Manchester Railway, the first steam railway to prove that goods and passengers could be carried in safety. This is yet another example of how open Canada is to the newest innovations in transportation and communication. Other examples include the latest in cabs being imported from London, the telegraph line stretching up the St Lawrence, and the experiments taking place on the roads with planks, with macadam, with improved ditching, and with other new vehicles, including a Russian droshky built especially for Lord Sydenham who had remembered them fondly from his years in St Petersburg. Yet, travel by land remains an arduous affair to be avoided if at all possible. Most of the roads are terrible. Streams, swamps, snow, and dark impenetrable forests overwhelm the would-be road

TEAMBOAT

Not every paddle-wheeler required fuel, nor was everyone
swept up by steam travel: some, such as the conservative
farmers near Quebec, preferred to remain closer to nature
as they spurned the noisy steam-ferries in favour of team-
boats when crossing the broad St Lawrence to Lévis. These
plump little boats were driven by two small side-paddles
activated by four horses walking round and round in the
centre of the open deck. (To increase the space available for
passengers and to reduce the amount required by the
horses, James McKenzie, owner of the Hotel McKenzie in
Lévis, designed his *Britannia* so that the horses worked in
a stationary position, walking on a drum.) Similar ferries
were still to be found elsewhere in the Canadas, including
two connecting with the United States: one plied the St
Lawrence between Prescott and Ogdensburgh, New York,
the other crossed the Niagara between Waterloo and Black
Rock, above the falls. In 1841 the Niagara ferry was replaced by a steamer which, it was predicted, would better
cope with ice and wind during the winter season.

TRAIN, CHAMPLAIN & ST LAWRENCE RAILWAY

The purpose of the Champlain & St Lawrence Railway was
to facilitate trade and communication between Lower
Canada and the United States. Since it crossed very flat terrain, little engineering was required except for a bridge
over the Little River, near L'Acadie, about six miles from
St John's. Before the railway was built, the route from
Montreal to St John's had been described as "nine miles by
water ... and the rest by mud." At times, no coach could attempt it and only the mail-wagons could hope to get
through. As on most Canadian roads, the hooves of the
horses and the wheels of the wagons constantly churned up
the surface, especially in the spring and the fall, frequently
making it impassable. In contrast, railways suffered little
damage from the passage of the locomotive and rail cars
and, although the initial cost might be high, maintenance
was relatively simple. However, when a problem did arise,
it was likely to be more serious because of the greater
complexity of the railway. For instance, early in October
1841, when the Little River Bridge was burned by an
"incendiary," service was disrupted for several days; two
weeks later the steamboat linking La Prairie with Montreal
struck a rock, causing further problems. In both cases,
troops were called in to help the private owners repair the
damage. The fire was thought to be "one of the fruits of
that bad feeling which is again showing itself in this
district." (An earlier unsuccessful attempt had been made
to destroy the same bridge during the disturbances of
1838.) A large reward of $1000 was offered by the
railway company for the "discovery and conviction of the
incendiary."

*The Dorchester,
Champlain
& St Lawrence
Railway.
Metropolitan
Toronto
Reference Library,
J. Ross Robertson
Collection, 4274*

builder who has little more to work with than a simple axe or a light drag. At best, his crude roads are not much more than sinuous paths twisting among the trees. Each spring they become heaving quagmires when the frost relinquishes its iron grip; summer, if dry, brings improved conditions; autumn, which is often wet, sees a reversion to the muddiness of spring; but winter, everyone agrees, is *the* season for travel by land: not only because water travel is no longer possible but also because the ground is frozen and blanketed with snow, providing perfect conditions for the easy circulation of sleighs, sleds, and toboggans.

Those living some distance from navigable waters depend on winter to convey their produce to market and to pick up their supplies of heavy goods such as potash kettles and liquor. It also provides an opportunity for settlers back in the bush to drive into town to procure clothing and fresh meat – a luxury they can seldom obtain in summer. Snow is an essential part of the annual cycle and a mild winter is regarded as a calamity.

Between Kingston and York by J.P. Cockburn. Watercolour, NAC

As soon as the ground is covered, vehicles of every description from stagecoach to wheelbarrow are placed on wooden runners shod with iron. Some carriage sleighs are well appointed and handsome; others, such as the market sleighs, are little more than two or three boards nailed together in the form of a box on runners; most are open but a few, like the four-horse mail stage between Kingston and Toronto, are covered. The most elegant sleighs are the cutters – essentially phaetons on high slender runners. Sported by the young men and officers of the garrison, they require considerable skill in driving.

Cutter. Winter Carriages, Quebec, 1842, by Mrs M.M. Chaplin. Detail, watercolour and pencil drawing, NAC

The French Canadians prefer their own little carioles. Unlike cutters, the runners are low. This might make them easier to handle but it also creates a problem in that snow is ploughed up in front of the dash. To surmount this impediment to speed, the driver rhythmically cracks his whip to send the horses into a series of sudden lurches, pulling the cariole up over the heaps of accumulated snow – leaving behind a trail lined with bumps or *cahots*. As winter drags on, the *cahots* grow larger and icier and become "an utter abomination to human feelings," shaking out

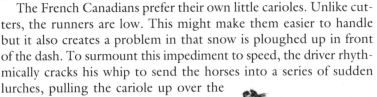

TELEGRAPH

The crossbeams of the telegraph had been a familiar fea-
ture on the Canadian horizon for several decades before
1841. By the raising of large wicker balls in certain combi-
nations, coded messages could be sent from one telegraph
station to the next, from the estuary of the St Lawrence up
river and on into the interior of Upper Canada. It was operated by the army and its role was primarily a military
one. However, it did perform other functions, such as let-
ting Quebec know in advance when immigrant and cargo
ships were approaching from down river.

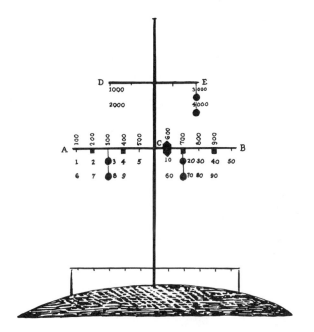

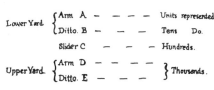

The Telegraph.
From
Telegraph,
Semaphore:
Description of,
and Instructions
for Its Use.
James Kempt, Qr.
Mr. Genl., BNA,
Ad. Qrs.
Québec, 1809, p. 2.
Redrawn
by Peter Ennals

MONTREAL CAB

London cabs of the latest fashion were among the innovations in transportation that found immediate acceptance in Canada. These handsome yellow vehicles first appeared in the streets of Montreal in April 1841. With a door at the rear, they could be backed into the sidewalk to enable passengers to enter and leave without stepping out into the muddy roadway. This arrangement meant that those inside had to sit sideways, facing one another. When the cab was in motion, the passengers jiggled back and forth, fully aware that should the horse suddenly rear, they would be in danger of being catapulted into the street. Nevertheless, the *Morning Courier* had nothing but praise for this latest novelty from England: it especially liked the protection provided against the weather and the stability afforded by the body of the vehicle being so close to the ground. All in all, the cab was "a decided improvement on the old ugly, awkward, and dangerous calèche."

In November another innovation, the closed-in sleigh, was to be seen on Montreal streets. It was described by the *Montreal Transcript* as being "as great an improvement on the former winter vehicles as the cabs have proved superior to the Calèche."

Montreal cab. Detail from a drawing of Notre Dame Street, Montreal. Metropolitan Toronto Reference Library, J. Ross Robertson Collection, 2836

"all loose teeth" and dislocating "uncompact joints." To overcome this nuisance, a sleigh ordinance was put into effect on 1 January 1841. It applied to all parts of Lower Canada except for the Quebec district, where it was restricted to mail routes.

Cariole.
Winter
Carriages,
Quebec, 1842,
by Mrs M.M.
Chaplin.
Detail,
watercolour and
pencil drawing,
NAC

The ordinance laid down in great detail how winter vehicles were to be constructed and the manner in which horses were to be attached to them. High runners were now mandatory, spelling the demise of the much loved cariole. Not surprisingly, the new rules fractured the brittle calm existing between English and French. Opponents of the ordinance have argued that it was unfair to compel 100,000 families who have "always used" winter carriages different from those prescribed to obtain new ones at an expense of some hundred thousand pounds – on pain of fine and punishment. Supporters of the ordinance have been quick to show their impatience with such arguments and, as usual, see behind the protest certain "leading characters who oppose everything, good or bad," who are stirring up the people against a measure "calculated as it is to improve the moral and social conditions of the French Canadian population." These characters would have one believe "that French Canadian prejudices are to be considered as equivalent to Acts of Parliament, as guaranteed by treaty, and must, therefore, be *respected.*"

Ordinance sleigh.
Sleighing in
the City
(my sleigh) of
Montreal by
H.J. Warre,
c. 1842.
Sepia wash,
NAC

Some of the heat which crept into the debate could be accounted for by the fact that the sleigh, especially for the French Canadian, is much more than a mere means of travel or a mode of transportation: during the long winter when little work can be done, sleighing for pleasure becomes the main form of recreation; and Jean-Baptiste is never happier than when he hitches his plucky little Canadian horse to his light, home-made cariole and races across the winter countryside. Sometimes he might stop to visit with friends; other times, it might be the church or the market; and although he takes great care to dress warmly in furs, frequent tavern stops seem necessary to insure that no frost-bite occurs. The whole atmosphere is one of great merriment, much increased by the happy jingle of sleigh bells. They, too, are required by law, but few who have followed them on a crisp winter's day are likely to protest.

The sleigh ordinance has been difficult to enforce and there are still complaints about roads continuing to be *cohoteuse*. For instance, two gentlemen who arrived in Quebec early in the new year from

ICE-BOATS AT QUEBEC

Ice-boat at Quebec.
Hauling Boats
by J.B. Wilkinson.
Watercolour
over graphite,
National
Gallery of Canada

Ice-boats kept Quebec in touch with Lévis on the south shore of the St Lawrence. Lévis was the terminus for routes from the lower provinces and from Boston. Tide, wind, broken ice, and snow storms made direct crossings all but impossible. Looking down from the noon-day gun, high in the Citadel, the boats were a single line of black ants picking their way across a white expanse. From the manner in which the line angled up or down river, it was not difficult to determine the flow of the tide. If there was a wind blowing, and there usually was, the boats would be forced still further off course. (Even the largely submerged pans of ice could be blown along at three or four knots.) With the wind came sudden snowstorms, or "whiteouts," which could obscure the distant shore, causing the boats to become lost. Thus it was not uncommon for the exhausted crews to touch land miles from their intended destination.

The ice-boats were very strong, being made from the hollowed-out trunks of a single tree or, as was more often the case, from two trunks, securely joined together. They were quite large and managed to carry as many as eight passengers in addition to a crew of three or four, not to mention the cargo which was securely lashed to the bottom.

The boats were paddled through open water and through small pieces of ice, but when a large pan was encountered it became necessary to bring out the drag ropes and the strong poles with the iron grappling hooks on the end, in order to wrestle the boat up onto the ice. A nimble foot was required as the men stepped onto the slippery, often rotting ice if a ducking were to be avoided. In order not to restrict movement, clothing that was both light and warm was worn. From time to time one of the men was unlucky enough to take a plunge. Rescue was generally immediate as his companions instantly grabbed and pulled him from the icy water and administered, with all possible speed, a *coupe de rum*, which was shared by both rescued and rescuers alike!

The ice-boats carried much of the food sold in the markets of the Lower Town of Quebec. No wonder there was cause for jubilation, about one year in ten, when the river froze over completely and sleighs could make the crossing. Not only did the trip become much safer but also much cheaper, greatly reducing prices – especially of bulky items such as hay and wood. The populace celebrated their delight by skating on the "pont," as the ice bridge was generally known.

Map of the Canadas showing waterways, canals, and remaining breaks in navigation

A glance at the map will show the places where interruptions to steamboat navigation still exist. These are at Sault Ste Marie (3 miles), between Lakes Erie and Ontario (28 miles), from Dickenson's Landing at the head of the Long Sault to Lake St Francis (11 1/4 miles), from Côteau-du-Lac to St Louis (12 miles), and from Lachine to Montreal (9 miles), making a total of 63 1/4 miles (Quebec Gazette, 1 October 1841). These obstacles to cheap commercial transportation have been partially removed through the construction of the Welland Canal (28 miles), the Cornwall Canal (11 1/4 miles), the locks at the Cedars and Cascades (12 miles), and by the Lachine Canal (9 miles), for a total of 60 1/4 miles (ibid.). The last three of these obstacles may also be avoided by using the Rideau Canal and the Ottawa River, with its own canals at Grenville, Chûte-à-Blondeau, and Carillon, and locks at Ste-Anne and Vaudreuil. This route is 245 miles (ibid.).

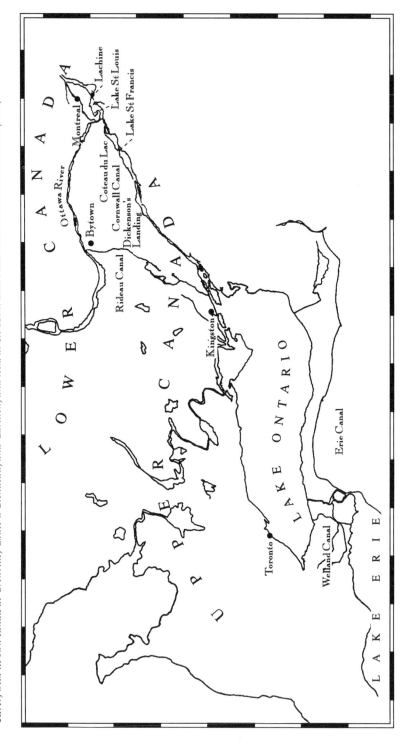

Boston by way of Montreal said they had met with no *cahots* until they came to Pointe-aux-Trembles. Meanwhile, another party – this time composed of more than 300 double sleighs manned by French Canadians – arrived from Rivière-du-Loup, 111 miles away. The sleds, loaded with provisions, had worked well until they reached the restriction-free road in the Quebec district. This bumpy track forms the last portion of the all-British winter route from Halifax to Quebec: it follows a line up the St John valley of New Brunswick, across the Temiscouata portage to Rivière-du-Loup on the St Lawrence, and along that river to Lévis, across the river from Quebec. The crossing to Quebec is completed by ice-boat.

The sleigh ordinance is only one example of how the "improving instinct," now sweeping the British Empire, can impinge upon the traditional ways of the "native" peoples under its care. For the British it seems only sensible to improve the winter roads by using the most modern means available; for the French Canadian it means a denial of his collective right to hold onto what is dear to him from the past. In any case, it showed how little is required to aggravate the underlying tensions which always exist between English and French in Canada.

Like other Scots of his time and place, Robertson was imbued with the "improving spirit." Yet he was reluctant to see the disappearance of some of the old ways, especially if they were being submerged by those imported from without. He was not at all happy with the increasing influence of London at the expense things Scottish, and so had some sympathy with his French-Canadian in-laws when they took a stand for the old-fashioned cariole against the modern ordinance sleigh. The sleigh ordinance provided just one illustration of the exotic nature of the spirit of improvement in the Canadas of the 1840s. It seemed to Robertson that the spirit had its origin in Great Britain and then diffused to the Canadas directly or by way of the United States.

The Inclined Plane – Quebec
James Pattison Cockburn
Musée du Séminaire de Québec

The inclined plane was a double-tracked, 600-foot railway that
ascended the citadel rock at a forty-five degree angle. It was used to convey large blocks
of stone and other building materials needed in the construction of the Citadel.

Chapter IV

The
Spirit
of
Improvement

Robertson was born in 1771, the year of publication in Edinburgh of the first edition of the Encyclopaedia Britannica, and grew up in the afterglow of the Scottish enlightenment that had thrown up men of great brilliance such as David Hume and Adam Smith. Although the giants were mostly gone, there were still eminent men to be encountered on their walks in The Meadows – men such as Lord Brougham, Lord Cockburn, and Lord Francis Jeffrey, to name but three. Words like "improving, improver and reformer" peppered their conversation – whether they were discussing education, criminal justice, medicine, agriculture, industry, or town planning. They knew that "improvements" came at a price and this, too, entered their discussions. Cockburn, especially, was upset because the building of the New Town had resulted in the destruction of some of the greenest meadows in Scotland. And, of course, they were all too aware that the rapid improvements in industry were displacing thousands of craftsmen, and that many of the advancements in agriculture were forcing thousands more, mostly crofters and agricultural labourers, off the land. Even some of the advances in medicine were taking place at the expense of robbed graves.

It was only natural that Robertson should continue to be interested in "improvements" during his stay in the Canadas. Once again, there is a large measure of *déjà vu* in his observations. The water carts of Quebec, for instance, reminded him of the "water caddies" of his youth, toting their loads on their backs and puffing up the steep circular stairs of old Edinburgh. Now, in Quebec, there was talk of introducing piped water – an improvement that had come to Edinburgh years earlier. Memories of the notorious Burke and Hare, who committed murder to supply corpses to one

of Edinburgh's great anatomists, were stirred when he met Edin-
burgh-trained James Douglas, one of the most respected doctors in
Quebec, who had been forced to flee to the United States two
decades earlier for dissecting corpses obtained clandestinely. In Edinburgh, Robertson had seen castings of the skulls of Burke and
Hare, made for phrenological study. In Quebec he discovered that
phrenology had just made its way to Canada. Robertson moved in
legal circles, among the advocates of Edinburgh who regarded
themselves as an important element in the city's aristocracy. This
accounts for his interest in the new penitentiary in Kingston.
It was here that he met Dr James Sampson, the prison's surgeon.
Robertson admired Sampson as an improver and mentions him
several times in this chapter.

Edinburgh was probably the leading medical centre in the
world, so it is not surprising that Robertson devotes considerable
space to hospitals and the treatment of disease in the Canadas. In
Scotland it was customary for the wealthy to travel to sunny, dry
climates, or to spas, for the amelioration of their health. Thus,
when Robertson's bad knee began acting up during his tour of the
Canadas, he decided on a side trip to newly established Caledonia
Springs on the Ottawa River. He reports on the spa in some detail.

Education was of importance to Robertson as it was to most
Scots. He, himself, had been behind the founding of the new Edinburgh Academy. For the most part, he favoured a classical education on the English model and was not impressed with the recent
Scottish trend towards the sciences. He ends his chapter on an encouraging note with the new Common Schools Act and the establishment of Queen's and Bishop's universities.

*A*lthough neither as advanced nor as strong as in Great Britain,
the spirit of improvement is now flourishing in the Canadas,
although not yet a robust growth. Possibly this is because it was not
germinated from native seed but rather from seed imported from the
mother country and the United States. It thrives best in English
Canada where, unlike French Canada, a similar language and way of
life have offered little resistance to its taking root. It has entered the
country in a myriad of ways: in instructions carried by colonial officials, with military officers, and as part of the baggage carried by the
thousands of immigrants who flood into the country each year. One
gentleman who is both an officer and an immigrant might be signaled for special mention as a carrier of the improving spirit. He is
James Sampson, the present mayor of Kingston, who came to Canada from England three decades ago.

Born in County Down, Dr Sampson was educated in Dublin before going to England to study medicine. In 1811 he was appointed assistant surgeon to the 85th Foot and was dispatched to Canada, where he took part in the War of 1812. After the war he was transferred to the 104th Foot at Quebec and Montreal. When his unit was disbanded in 1817 he went on half pay. For a short time he lived in Niagara and Queenston, before settling into civilian practice in Kingston.

In countless ways Sampson has assisted in the diffusion of the spirit of improvement in Canada: to promote better farming, he has taken on several high offices in the Midland District Agricultural Society and has made available free wheat and prize cattle from his own experimental farm. To improve transportation to markets, he became a commissioner for the improvement of the St Lawrence. To ameliorate the medical profession, he has examined and trained medical students and has been an active member of the Medical Board of Upper Canada for two decades. One could go on but perhaps it would be more useful to examine in some detail the general responses to three concerns of Dr Sampson: the treatment of the sick, the insane, and the convicted.

In 1832 Sampson was one of the three commissioners appointed by the Assembly of Upper Canada to superintend the building of a charity hospital for the poor of Kingston. This was to replace the

Dr James Sampson, mayor of Kingston. Queen's University Archives

Kingston General Hospital. Queen's University Archives

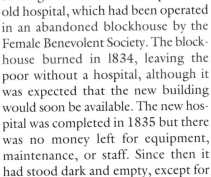

old hospital, which had been operated in an abandoned blockhouse by the Female Benevolent Society. The blockhouse burned in 1834, leaving the poor without a hospital, although it was expected that the new building would soon be available. The new hospital was completed in 1835 but there was no money left for equipment, maintenance, or staff. Since then it had stood dark and empty, except for a few months during the troubles of 1837–38, when it was occupied by the militia. In 1841, when Lord Sydenham was casting about for a suitable site for the first sitting of the first parliament of the newly united Canadas, its presence proved to be an enticement. The fact that the building was available and could be converted to a parliament building at little expense was important in the governor general's arriving at his decision to choose Kingston as the capital.

In spite of the fact that money for its construction had come through the efforts of a citizens' committee and a grant from the Upper Canadian legislature, there were few grumbles when the empty hospital was appropriated by the government. Why would there be? When sick, the rich knew they would be well attended at home, and the poor, for whom all hospitals are intended, live in fear of some time being sent there. That hospitals are free and that doctors who practise in them give their services gratuitously only adds to the anxiety for, as objects of public charity, patients are expected to contribute to the general welfare by enabling doctors to train. Perhaps this is only fair, but to the poor it seems like experimentation and there have been rumours that dissection is the ultimate goal of the medical attendants.

Like others elsewhere, the Kingston hospital stands on a large lot away from the town where the circulation of air is good and the land is cheap. (Cemeteries occupy similar positions and, in the minds of some, the number of return journeys is also alike.) In keeping with the modern stress on the benefits of fresh air, its ceilings are high and verandas are provided on each of the three floors of the handsome stone building.

The only other civilian hospital in Upper Canada, the Toronto General, has also run into money problems and was forced to close its doors early in 1841 amidst hints that its funds have been mismanaged. Unlike hospitals in the old country, the Toronto General was free only for paupers – and no more than twenty of these could *Old General* be provided for at one time. Other patients were expected to pay a *Hospital, Toronto.* shilling a day, except those in the Lock Ward (for syphilis), who *Metropolitan* were charged an extra sixpence. (They were kept apart not only to *Toronto* protect the morals of the other patients, especially the young, from *Reference Library,* being corrupted but also so they could be in a setting where the *J. Ross Robertson* means of reformation might be sedulously applied.) *Collection, 908*

Subscribers to the Toronto General, and clergymen in congregations making collections for its support, were allowed to recommend patients but it had been up to the medical attendants to rule on whether they were to be admitted. The insane, the incurable, and idiots were not to be admitted. Nor were women in advanced pregnancy: the high death rate among mothers in lying-in hospitals is becoming well known, and the meanest home is a far safer place to give birth.

In an age increasingly aware that illness often spreads from the poor to the rich, hospitals provide a unique opportunity for combining Christian charity with self-interest. Supporters of the Toronto General have argued that its closing will add to the misery of sick and homeless immigrants who were crowding into the city each summer. It will also remove a convenient place for disposing of sick servants who might otherwise infect the whole household. Servants in hospital did not have to be housed and fed by their masters during the period of inactivity but, to prevent abuse, masters who had been subscribers to the hospital were allowed to send their servants as patients so long as they paid a shilling per day for subsistence in addition to the amount subscribed. The continuance of the hospital is seen as a necessary aid for the medical school, which is likely to be established at the university. In the small compass of the hospital the medical student would see far more practice than by going around to the houses of the sick. The time saved could be applied to reading and other studies.

Meanwhile, in Montreal, where three students graduated from the new McGill medical school in May 1841, three hospitals are flourishing. The newest is the Montreal General, founded in 1818 by the Protestant Ladies' Benevolent Society as a House of Recovery for those suffering from contagious fevers. In 1822 it became a general hospital and moved into a new and larger building. Since then a further addition has been made possible through a large gift from a wealthy Montreal merchant, John Richardson. Although perhaps the first example of such munificence in Canada, many hospitals in Great Britain and the United States have been the beneficiaries of similar philanthropy from rising merchants and industrialists. Besides donations, the Montreal General is supported by subscriptions and by grants from the legislature. Patients are about equally divided between Protestants and Catholics.

To allay the distrust of hospitals in the public mind, the returns of admissions, discharges, and deaths at some institutions are regularly published in the newspapers. The new Marine Hospital at Quebec, for example, during the active season between 1 May and 30 November 1841, admitted 1352 patients. Of these, 1273 were discharged, 37 died, and 42 remained in hospital. The most common complaints were fever (406), syphilis (141), and rheumatism (134). The hospital is intended primarily for sailors and others who arrive by sea. During the 1841 season 899 sailors, 370 immigrants, and 83 townspeople were admitted. There were also 205 out-door patients.

Construction on the Marine Hospital building was begun in 1832 and was sufficiently completed in 1834 to begin taking patients. It is a very modern building with flues and machinery for conveying foul air to the roof. These would be less necessary had the design of the building been more concerned with cross-ventilation and less with classical proportions – it is said that the proportions were taken from the Temple of the Muses on the Ilissus near Athens. Running

Marine Hospital, Quebec, from an original by A.J. Russell. Hawkins's Pictures of Quebec with Historical Recollections (Quebec 1834), facing p. 261, NAC

water is installed. Drawn from the nearby St Charles River, it is filtered before being conducted to storage tanks at the top of the building. This is probably just as well since the Roman Catholic Hôpital Général is only a short distance further up-stream. Hot and cold baths were installed on each floor "for those who required them."* The upper storey was planned as a separate lying-in hospital for thirty-four patients. With room for a total of 362 patients, the Marine Hospital is fairly large. In Great Britain and elsewhere it has been discovered that the larger the hospital, the higher the death-rate among the mothers. That is probably why the lying-in hospital is not presently in use.

* Although considered a powerful remedy in many cases of disease, baths were not much used in private homes in Canada, even by people in decent circumstances, because of the inconvenience in providing them. Montreal alone had running water, and then only in the wealthier areas.

The healing power of nature is increasingly recognized as an essential handmaiden in the process of recovery. Thus the Marine Hospital was purposefully located outside the city in the countryside so that patients might profit from the fine views of the rivers and mountains. There are also extensive gardens and ornamental grounds where convalescent patients can enjoy fresh air and exercise. The healing views across the St Lawrence and St Charles are somewhat mitigated by the unhappy presence of two adjacent cholera burying-grounds, one Protestant, the other Catholic. Although separated in death, patients in life are admitted to the hospital without distinction. In so doing the Marine Hospital is following in the tradition of the venerable Roman Catholic hospitals which, from the battles of the Plains, have cared for all who have come to their gates, regardless of creed or language.

Hôtel Dieu, Montreal, 1829 by J.P. Cockburn. Print, NAC

Hôpital générale, Quebec. Metropolitan Toronto Reference Library, J. Ross Robertson Collection, 917.144 B594 opp.83

The Catholic hospitals in Quebec and Montreal are among the oldest in all the Americas. By 1644, within the walls of each settlement, there was an "Hôtel-Dieu," as the principal hospital in French towns and cities was known. By the time the Hôpital Général at Quebec and the Hôpital Général at Montreal were founded fifty years later, conditions in the colony were such that the new hospitals could be safely built outside the walls, where they could benefit from fresh air and abundant supplies of clean water from nearby rivers.

All the hospitals were under the care of nuns. (The Hôpital Général at Montreal was founded by brothers for the care of male patients only but later was taken over by the Grey Nuns, who expanded its scope.) The sisters are universally admired and extravagantly praised by men such as Walter Henry (a Protestant doctor), who rhapsodized: "I love French Nuns.

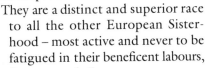

They are a distinct and superior race to all the other European Sisterhood – most active and never to be fatigued in their beneficent labours, and of pure morals."

Few important visitors have departed from Canada without visiting the Catholic hospitals. Many have left accounts of the cleanliness, orderliness, and freshness they saw as well as descriptions of the devotion of the nuns, whose kindliness, gentleness, and goodwill contribute at least as much to the patients' care as the medicines administered. (Some have been surprised to learn that the sisters at the Hôtel-Dieu are cloistered and were impressed that none had "escaped" even though the gates were open every day.) Relieving one another every two hours, day and night, the sisters take turns in attending the sick. When time permits, they do embroidery and other handwork which is sold to augment hospital funds. Other sources of income vary from hospital to hospital but they include revenues derived from seigneurial lands, grants from the provincial assembly, and donations. The Hôpital Général at Montreal received a grant from the French government that continued even after the Conquest.

During the first half-century of British rule both English and French relied on the Catholic hospitals, but as the towns grew and immigrants poured in the hospitals could no longer cope. Montreal responded to the increasing need with the building of the Montreal General Hospital and Quebec with the Marine Hospital. As is implied by their name, the Hôtel-Dieu hospitals in both Quebec and Montreal are intended to do God's work in caring for the sick and the poor. This mandate has continued into the present and the Catholic hospitals continue to accept, in addition to acute patients, the aged and chronically ill. The Hôpital Général at Montreal also takes care of destitute children until they are old enough to support themselves.

The new "English" hospitals are inspired by a different philosophy and do not knowingly admit chronic-care patients. Thus the turnover of patients is quite rapid and larger numbers can be cared for.

Unlike the new hospitals, the French Catholic hospitals take in the insane, although there appears to be little attempt to effect a cure. It is disturbing to hear the screams from the attic of the Hôtel Dieu or from the isolation cells of the Hôpital Général at Quebec. The cells are overcrowded and there is no ventilation. The odour is so unbearable that visitors can remain for only a few moments and, of course, the insane suffer terribly.

The Hôpital Général in Montreal also takes in the insane but, late in 1841, "for want of a more suitable place twenty-four lunatics" were locked up in the Common Gaol. Out of necessity, many others are being kept at home, where they are a burden on their families, or are to be seen wandering up and down the country in destitution and hopeless misery.

The situation is no better in Upper Canada. In Kingston, lunatics are being confined with the prisoners in the new penitentiary. For James Sampson, who is the prison's surgeon, this is wrong and he is fighting to have the insane segregated from the convicts. He is also opposed to the accepted practice of public viewing of the inmates and wants an end to punishment of the insane. There is, however, reason to hope for improvement in the care of the insane. A commission was appointed in 1839 – Sampson is a member – to erect a provincial lunatic asylum.

THE NEED FOR AN ASYLUM

The need for an asylum – a protected place for those unable to care for themselves – was becoming more apparent to an increasingly enlightened population. Here the lunatic would be able to receive the soothing remedies, cheerfulness, and repose that would alleviate and, perhaps, remove his symptoms. Many types of mental derangement were recognized and there was much speculation on their various causes. These ranged from too violent mental exertion to the after effects of the many gloomy, poorly educated preachers who wandered through the country shaking the nerves of young innocent women with their doctrines of eternal punishment. Its cause might not be clear, but insanity was being treated with greater compassion and there was a growing awareness that it was an illness – an illness that could be cured.

The crime rate of Upper Canada has not been high during the past decade but there is a perception among the upper classes that the lower ranks are getting out of hand. The latter are not as cowed as they might have been in the old country, thanks to the prevailing "levelling influence." Indeed, at times the whole social order seemed threatened. A solution was sought by looking to the mother country and the United States, where the improving spirit had led to the founding of penitentiaries. A place was needed where the lower ranks might be imbued with habits of regularity and industry – a place where prisoners would do beneficial work and learn a trade so that they would return to the community as useful citizens.

The current system of criminal justice has not been working well. The death penalty is not being applied in cases less than murder; fines are considered unjust since they favour those with means; local jails only increase crime since young offenders are lumped in with

PENITENTIARY

The notion that criminals could be "cured" or reformed
was also gaining acceptance. The idea had its roots
in a belief propagated by the English philanthropist and
prison reformer John Howard that crime was the result
of an evil environment. His two-volume *Prisons and
Lazarettos* was published in 1777 during the decade when
the American colonies were no longer available for the
transportation of prisoners from Great Britain but before
convict settlements were established in Australia. Other
ways had to be found to deal with the mounting numbers
of prisoners who were then clogging British jails and filling up the prison hulks anchored around the coast.
The time was ripe for considering the ideas put forth by
Howard. His system would not only punish the prisoner
but would also reform them through a strict regime of
behaviour control. He advocated that "the hours of rising,
of reading a chapter in the Bible, of prayers, of meals,
of work, etc. should all be fixed by the magistrates, and
notice of them given by a bell ... To reform prisoners,
or to make them better as to their morals, should be the
leading view in every house of correction, and their
earnings should only be a *secondary* object."

Howard's theories were based on his observations during
a tour on the continent. These in turn were taken up and
refined by reformers in Great Britain, the United States,
and ultimately Canada. The instrument of reform was not
a jail but a penitentiary. Derived from the word "penitence," the penitentiary was to be a place where the prisoner, through contemplation and reading his Bible, would
repent of his sins and amend his life. Though not unduly
harsh, conditions would be sufficiently unpleasant to
discourage the repetition of misdeeds and to dissuade others from committing crimes.

seasoned criminals; corporal punishment is increasingly regarded as improper and degrading, and banishment is often unenforceable in a continent where it is so easy to move about.

The architectural plan for the new penitentiary at Kingston is very elaborate. Tiny cells are arranged in tiered rows in cell blocks that radiate from a central rotunda. This configuration, along with inspector's corridors containing peepholes, makes supervision easy and gives the prisoner the impression that he is being watched at all times. When completed, the penitentiary will accommodate more than 800 prisoners. Although intended only for Upper Canada, it will now serve the whole country.

The designers of the penitentiary have drawn heavily from the United States, where two methods of prison discipline are being promoted: the Philadelphia system and the Auburn system. In the Philadelphia system prisoners are kept in solitary confinement at all times. This not only prevents older prisoners from teaching their evil ways to younger inmates but it insures adequate time for repentance and protects the prisoner's identity. Reformed criminals when released would not even recognize one another should they pass on the street. In the Auburn system prisoners are confined separately at night but work together by day. No contact or conversation is allowed between them. When taking their meals they sit so as not to see the faces of the prisoners opposite them. Both systems stress hard work and silence. Kingston has drawn heavily on the Auburn Penitentiary and to a lesser extent on Sing Sing, which follows a similar regime.

Kingston Penitentiary has also been influenced by the work of the Boston Prison Discipline Society, which believes that the penitentiary can make up for the lack of parental guidance by providing a disciplined setting for the prisoner. As with John Howard before it, the society stresses the importance of the design of the prison building. "Moral architecture" is advocated – architecture that draws inspiration from the order and harmony of classical models. Thus, on entering Kingston Penitentiary through the Doric columns on either side of the gate the new prisoner is immediately confronted with the classical proportions of the main building. Lifting his eyes he sees the elegant, windowed dome capping the central rotunda. The dome is not designed merely to provide light and air but is intended to be pleasing to the eye. The Boston Prison Discipline Society has suggested that the same principles of architecture could be beneficially applied to boarding schools, almshouses, and seminaries – especially those intended for the lower ranks of society.

The penitentiary is intended as a model to society as a whole – rational, disciplined, and self-supporting. Trades such as ropemaking, shoemaking, blacksmithing, tailoring, and stonecutting are taught and the goods produced by the prisoners are intended for outside sale to cover expenses. However, the prison's income from these sources has not been large and local tradesmen complain about unfair competition.

As at Auburn where admission is charged, visitors are admitted to the penitentiary.* To the casual visitor there is every indication that the institution is working well, but James Sampson, who makes regular visits in his capacity as surgeon, knows otherwise. Under the administration of the warden, Henry Smith, unduly harsh punishment is being used to make the prisoners conform. Floggings with the cat-o'nine-tails are common even for minor infractions. The floggings are carried out in front of other prisoners. Sampson opposes the opening of the penitentiary to idle sightseers, but he has encouraged local groups to send visitors into the prison. Among these is a lady much filled with the spirit of improvement, Harriet Dobbs Cartwright, of the Female Benevolent Society. She was one of the first regular visitors to the prison and has been especially distressed by the incarceration of female lunatics. Sampson, himself, has assisted prisoners after their release.

Late in June 1841 Sampson and his medical colleagues were faced with an epidemic of dysentery. No fewer than thirty members of the Lower House of Parliament were rumoured to have been laid low. The cause was probably the town's drinking water, which is drawn from the harbour where there is no current to disperse the filth of the town. In November the situation was improved somewhat when an enterprising townsman placed a large cast-iron pump at the end of his wharf within range of the current. The pump is capable of raising 100 gallons a minute to a cistern where it is filtered before being taken away by carters to all parts of the town. The water situation at Kingston is typical of all Canadian towns and cities. It is known that illness is more common in the cities than in the countryside and it is thought that an inadequate supply of clean water might be a cause. Moreover, without a reliable source of water, devastating fires are all too prevalent in the towns. (Kingston, alone, lost 158 buildings in a single fire in 1840, and another huge loss was suffered by Quebec in 1841.) The need for better water supplies is obvious. But who will pay for it?

---

* Not all were idle sightseers. Some, like Charles Dickens, who would visit the prison in 1842, were genuinely interested in the welfare of the prisoners.

The same arguments of self-interest that have been used to persuade the rich to support the building of hospitals for the poor are now being enlisted to persuade them also to support the creation of public water systems. Would-be improvers point out that fevers often originate in the crowded quarters of the poor and from there spread to the homes of the rich. Surely it is in the interest of the rich, who would bear most of the cost of public water-works, to enable the poor to clean up their homes and themselves, and so reduce this noisome source of disease. Fires, too, spread from poor areas to rich, and a ready source of water would not only protect all homes but would reduce the high rates of insurance. Although no Canadian town has a municipal water supply, Montreal has the best arrangement. Water from the river is pumped by a steam-engine to a cistern on Citadel Hill. From this reservoir, it flows through cast iron pipes buried below the frost-line. The work is the private undertaking of a Scottish immigrant and water is available to subscribers only. Other Montrealers are still dependent on wells or water-carts.

In Quebec there were 950 wells at the end of 1841. About half of these are in the St Johns ward. Crowded St Roch has to make do with only 196 – and most of these are actually sumps that are intended only for draining water from cellars. Similarly in the Lower Town, which is strung along the river, residents can actually follow the rise and fall of the changing tides merely by looking into one of the thirty-three wells.

Petulant carter. The Jesuit Barracks and Market, Quebec, 1829 by J.P. Cockburn. Print, NAC

Carts collecting water from the St Lawrence and its tributary, the St Charles, wait for the extreme ebb of the tide to ensure getting only fresh water from up river. However, since the outfall from the sewers and other filth is carried up river on the tide, there is always the possibility of harvesting it on the way down. The large number of water-carriers – 112 in 1841 – is a good indicator of the low quality of well water. Like carters everywhere, they are noted for their petulance as they manoeuvre their sloshing loads up hill along the narrow, winding, crowded streets. When they learned of the proposals being made late in the year for the regulation of their trade, they undoubtedly profaned many of the sacred words learned in church. From now on tubs are to be of a certain size and so constructed that water will not spill onto the roads, causing mud or ice, or giving a surprise dousing to unsuspecting pedestrians. Water spilled, of course, means short measure for the buyer.

Water is carried to all parts of the city, even to the extensive estates of the more opulent families in the St Louis suburb on the Plains of Abraham. Like many Quebeckers, they use carted water for the table, and water from their own wells for washing dishes and other culinary purposes.

Water in these higher parts of the city is usually impure because the thin layer of earth over the clay-slate rocks does

Carrying Water in Winter by Mrs M.M. Chaplin. Watercolour, NAC

not allow surface water to be adequately filtered before entering the wells. The most highly regarded table water is taken from three sites along the St Charles near the Hôpital Général and the Marine Hospital. Other water is taken from near the mouth of the St Charles and from the St Lawrence in the Lower Town. Sewers carrying filth from houses and cesspools, and wastes from factories, discharge into both rivers. The mouths of three or four of the principal sewers are at the very points where water is procured by the carriers. Carts and teams are hurriedly backed into the shallow rivers, stirring up mud and débris, which is carried off as part of the load. Both the St Charles and St Lawrence are used as dumps. Even the garrison regularly marches down to the bateaux wharf "in a silent, proper manner" to empty their straw-mattresses into the river.

Toronto Harbour. Fish-Market, Toronto by W.H. Bartlett. In Willis, Canadian Scenery, vol. 1, facing p. 88

At Montreal, washer-women do their laundry beside the loading carts. At Toronto there are complaints of all manner of filth – including dead animals – being dumped on the harbour ice in winter, only to fall into the harbour in spring. At certain seasons there is much illness. Many families flee to Niagara for two or three days at a time – for a change of air.

That people flee for a "change of air" is a reflection of the widely held theory that most diseases are airborne. Water is seldom suspect, although it is believed that certain dissolved minerals – especially limestone – can produce diarrhoea. Water containing other impurities is rejected as unpalatable rather than unsafe; tainted well water is acceptable for washing dishes but not for drinking. Water from the St Lawrence causes in most strangers a disagreeable looseness and it is generally recommended that the water be mixed with wine or spirits – or even boiled – until the body becomes accustomed to it. The lime in the water is thought to be the cause of its aperient effect.

It has frequently been observed that the amount of sickness is greater in summer than in winter, but no connection has been drawn between the use of water from the rivers in summer and from melted snow in winter. The increase is usually attributed to the effects of the warm sun acting on the filth in the streets to produce "noxious effluvia" or "miasmas" that can taint the air for some distance. Tainted air is believed to be the source of many diseases. Not all miasmas can be attributed to man or his works. Some have natural origins. For instance, the malodorous air emitted by swampy land is known to be, as it has been for centuries, the cause of intermittent fevers known, variously, as "ague," "swamp-fever," or "alternating-fever." During the 1820s a British doctor introduced into English the Italian term, "malaria" (*mal'aria* – bad air) for the swamp emissions, and "malaria fever" for the diseases they cause.

Ague, as it is usually known in Canada, is widespread in Upper Canada but almost unknown in Lower Canada – a curiosity that has caused much speculation. Is it because the lands of Lower Canada have been longer settled and better drained, and so have ceased to give off noxious effluvia? Is it because the climate is cooler and the snow lies longer on the ground? Why is ague rare in the forest and in newly cleared lands during the first season, and why are most settlers first attacked during their second year? Is it because the settlers persist in drinking stagnant water and exposing themselves to the noon-day sun and the night air, as some say; or is it really because they are subjected to the exhalations of the newly exposed soils? Whatever the reason, everyone knows that ague abounds, and that it is encountered with increasing frequency and severity as one travels from the Ottawa River to the shores of Lake Erie.

All lakes and marshes are looked on as sources of malaria but none more so than the notorious Cranberry Marsh between the Rideau Lakes and Lake Ontario. The Rideau Canal passes through the marsh – a circumstance that has caused travellers to use it in fear or to avoid it in favour of the St Lawrence route. Much of the canal was constructed by building a series of dams to form a line of connecting lakes. This has resulted in a great deal of "drowned land," which has added to the canal's unwholesome reputation – a reputation justly attained during the construction period when hundreds of workers were stricken with ague and many died from its effects. The large number of deaths resulted in part from the difficult living conditions of the men, many of whom were immigrants already weakened by hardship or from drink. Some were said to have been victims of yellow fever, although it is possible that this disease was confused with another with similar symptoms.

Settlers are cautioned to avoid malarial areas and to choose for their houses sites that are high to ensure that cellars will be dry. Yet,

THE MOSQUITO

The mosquito was a great annoyance but it was not suspected as being a carrier of ague or of any other disease. (That malaria was mosquito borne would not be known until the end of the century.) Troops were frequently transferred to Canada from the tropical regions of the empire and may have contributed to the incidence of malaria and possibly of yellow fever. (The troop ship *Apollo* was only five weeks out of Jamaica when it arrived at Quebec in August 1841.) Improved transportation was enabling more people to travel further and faster than ever before. It was also permitting diseases formerly confined to restricted parts of the globe to migrate to new lands. The most ghastly of these exotics to reach Canada before 1841 was without question the Asiatic cholera.

even with this precaution, ague is common after the first year and, because its incidence is greatest just when the work is heaviest, it has greatly retarded the progress of settlement. Fortunately the death-rate is low and after a few years most settlers seem to become immune or, as they would say, "acclimated to the location." Sulphate of quinine is used both as a preventative and as a cure. In keeping with the contemporary passion for purges, it is often supplemented with calomel, castor-oil, and salts.

Cholera Plague, Quebec
by Joseph Légaré.
Oil on canvas, National Gallery of Canada

Cholera first reached Canada in 1832 and quickly made its way into the interior along the waterways. The only settled area of any size to escape was the relatively isolated Eastern Townships of Lower Canada. The unusually large number of immigrants, the widespread use of steamboats, and the crowded poor near the docks in most towns all appeared to contribute to its rapid spread.* Some believed the disease to be contagious while others believed it to be a result of miasmas. As a consequence, there were a variety of responses. Some people chose to flee to the country while others considered it safe to remain in town. A quarantine station was set up below Quebec at Grosse-Ile for ships entering the Canadas. Yet passengers from ships without illness had been frequently mixed with others who were sick. Throughout the colony, cholera patients were isolated in special hospitals – and those who died were sent to separate cholera burying-grounds. Troops were generally confined to barracks. Following the epidemic of 1832 and another in 1834, a number of municipal bylaws were passed which reflect the thinking of the miasmatists. They are concerned with the regulation of sources of noxious effluvia such as drains, filth, privies, and public markets, and the provision of a better circulation of air. Judging from the continued filth of the streets and inns – especially in old Quebec and Montreal – it would seem that the bylaws have not been very

* Food and drink, usually water, contaminated with feces from cholera patients or carriers were the means of transmission, but this was unknown to doctors in the 1830s, who were confounded by the disease.

effective. In newer settlements, such as Bytown [Ottawa], where the streets are wide and laid out in a regular pattern, good air is more easily achieved.

Approximately one-half of the cholera victims died. Bereaved men could usually take care of themselves but widows with young children and orphans were often reduced to poverty and so became objects of charity. However, poverty and hardship have by no means been limited to the families of cholera victims. Even today, many poor people resort to the streets and there is much concern about the large number of beggars, including children. According to the social reformer James Silk Buckingham, the situation is quite different from that in the United States, where he had seen no American beggars during a tour of three years. Buckingham made his comment after being descended upon by several beggars during his first five minutes in Toronto. This happened in 1840 – three years after the establishment of a House of Refuge and Industry that was intended to correct this evil.

Like the penitentiary, the House of Refuge and Industry is based on the notion that people, particularly the idle poor, can be improved and made into useful members of society. Its supporters believed that it would lead to the end of street begging as well as to the prevention of juvenile crime. They also view it as a means of rescuing the deserving poor from misery and degradation, and of restoring them to happiness and usefulness.* The Toronto House of Industry and Refuge is supported by subscriptions, grants from the city council and the legislature, and by the modest proceeds from the labour of the inmates. Inmates' earnings are low because too few citizens have called upon their services; these include the washing of clothes, sewing, and doing various things for tradesmen and manufacturers requiring little skill. Most of those helped have been out-door pensioners who receive food, fire-wood, and, where possible, clothing. Those actually staying in the house are mostly widows, children, and old or infirm men.

Some of the urchins still to be seen begging in the streets of Toronto are actually from families who have been receiving relief. To correct this abuse of charity, there are those who advocate that parents should be made to consent to having their children apprenticed before aid is granted to the family. Ideally, children would be

---

* Not everyone was imbued with the spirit of improvement. Such idealism escaped the *Kingston Chronicle and Gazette*. Early in 1841 it called for a similar House of Industry at Kingston, where "the vicious and profligate might be committed."

taken from their parents and apprenticed in some place far removed from the temptations of the city. It is generally accepted that the corrupting influence of the city can be corrected by the restorative qualities of the countryside.

In 1841 Toronto required an additional House of Refuge and Industry. It was suggested that it be established on one or two hundred acres, preferably with a mill-stream, five or ten miles from the city. With such a house in place, providing for the needs of the destitute, the unprotected, and the youthful delinquent, citizens would be quite justified in putting a complete stop to all street-begging. Montreal, Quebec, and various cities in the United States also have houses of industry where inmates are exposed to an atmosphere of discipline designed to reform their habits and fit them for usefulness.

Poverty is now generally regarded as a social problem that can be corrected. Its main cause, according to the committee for the relief of the poor and destitute in Toronto, is intemperance, and the committee recommends that "a barrier should be placed in the way of a gratification of a desire for intoxicating liquors, by *the steady refusal of pecuniary relief,* and by bestowing other kinds of it only as a reward for labour performed – cases of sickness excepted." Intemperance is also the root of much crime and the downfall of a majority of prisoners in both the Kingston Penitentiary and the Quebec City jail and, probably, in other prisons as well.

Drunkenness is a common cause of death in this land where thousands are adjusting not only to much colder winters and much hotter summers, but also to an accelerating pace of life. Accidents are common as men strike feet with axes, fall overboard from steamers or freeze to death in the streets. At Quebec, alone, the coroner held inquests for no fewer than thirty-nine persons who had died as a result of drunkenness between March and September 1840. Yet, in his opinion, this did not represent a third of those who perished from the same cause during the same period.

Drink is very cheap in Canada, especially in comparison with Great Britain, and it is a great temptation to the poor immigrant who is coping with the harsh reality of pioneer life. Vast quantities of hard liquor are imported from the mother country, the West Indies, and elsewhere. Oceans more are produced in Canada.

Beer is not much used here, partly because it sells for as much (or as little!) as spirits. Barley, the basic ingredient of beer, does not do well in virgin soils of the frontier. It is not highly regarded for malting, and beer brewed from Canadian malt is seldom good. The great fluctuations in temperature, in comparison with Great Britain, add to the difficulties in malting. Spirits, unlike beer, can be made from a number of grains which *do* do well in Canada, including wheat and, especially, rye. Beer has a much shorter life than spirits and, because it is bulkier and more subject to freezing, it is not easily transported in this vast and frigid land. Most of it is consumed in the towns where it is brewed, leaving the countryside almost entirely to spirits.

Grog shop in Quebec. St John Street from the corner of Palace Street by J.P. Cockburn. Detail, watercolour, pen and ink over pencil, Royal Ontario Museum

Many Canadians consider beer to be wholesome and spirits trash. Others fail to make this distinction and regard most of the many beer shops as nothing but drunkeries of the worst character. For the poor migrants, sailors, and soldiers, any drinking place is a welcome relief from grinding despair. Wherever these people are concentrated in large numbers, as in the Lower Town of Quebec, numerous taverns and grog shops are to be found. That taverns and poverty go hand in hand is obvious, but most reformers, including temperance advocate James Silk Buckingham, see excessive drinking as the cause and not the effect of extreme poverty and degradation. That consumption is high is vividly illustrated by the final line of an advertisement intended for the general public inserted by a new brewery in Quebec: "Customers whose consumption is small will be furnished with casks containing 7 1/2 gallons."

Buckingham toured the Canadas in 1839 to deliver a series of lectures on his travels in the Holy Lands – and to puff the cause of temperance. Widely regarded as one of the finest speakers of our time, his travel lectures were heard by capacity audiences in Toronto, Kingston, Montreal, and Quebec. His temperance lectures, in which he advocated total abstinence, were less well received. Temperance and travel talks were interspersed and attendance fluctuated with the subject discussed. Community leaders, including the lieutenant-governor, the chief justice, and other dignitaries, came to the travel lectures but were conspicuously absent on the nights when temperance was being advocated. This greatly distressed Buckingham. Like other reformers and improvers, he feels that it is the duty of the upper classes to provide a model that others might emulate. If only they would support the cause, through precept and example, the lower classes could be elevated from misery and degradation and rescued from their follies and crimes.

The notion that members of the upper classes should be models of decorum for the lower classes is not widely held by those at the pinnacle of society in the Canadas. Lord Sydenham himself was, before his untimely death, criticized for not living an exemplary life. Worldly men like Sir Richard Bonnycastle are irritated by temperance advocates, whom he regards as obscure individuals who seek to attain "a pseudo celebrity, without the previous acquirements of education, observation, and research." Like religious converts, they make great merit of their conversion and "the cause" becomes their drink; like other converts they are sometimes trapped in their own rhetoric. A Mr Bentley is such a person: at a meeting of the Quebec Young Men's Total Abstinence Society in March he became so carried away that in his attempt to make a public display of his knowledge of the scriptures, "he introduced matters of the greatest indelicacy which almost had the effect of compelling every female present to retire."

Temperance and religion are becoming increasingly intertwined but most congregations are still composed of both adherents and non-adherents of the cause. Buckingham was freely offered the use of Methodist churches in Toronto, Kingston, and Montreal for his lectures, but at Quebec the same denomination would allow the use of its building only with the understanding that no meeting in favour of temperance would be held there. The condition was exacted, against the will of the minister, by some of the trustees of the chapel who are distillers and dealers in ardent spirits. This was unacceptable to Buckingham, who moved his series first to the Court House, then to the Theatre Royal, before finally settling in the Hall of the Legislative Assembly, where he addressed his audiences from the speaker's chair. Buckingham was more successful in Quebec than elsewhere in drawing members of the upper classes to his temperance lectures. On the final evening the commander of the garrison had a large body of Coldstream Guards marched to the legislature, where they learned about the evils of alcohol while sitting in the strangers' gallery.

Military bands are now being enlisted in the cause of temperance. When the Friends of Temperance of Montreal recently held a steamboat excursion, the band of the 85th Regiment was permitted by its officers to go along. Over 300 passengers embarked; during the day they visited several villages, ending at St Sulpice where a temperance meeting was held. The only beverage on board was pure water, with "an abundance of ice." In August the Grenadier Guards band took part in a similar cruise of the Quebec Young Men's Total Abstinence Society. Groups such as these stress the importance of taking "the pledge" against drinking. This is done in the atmosphere of charged emotion that often follows temperance meetings. The temperance cause belongs to the men, although women, sometimes intemperate themselves and often the victims of drunken men, have taken more than a passing interest in it, attending outings and meetings. Women are the weaker vessel and the Female Benevolent Society of Kingston was quite exceptional in venturing "so far out of place as to get up a petition to the magistrates to diminish the licenses and look after the unlicensed dram shops abounding in every quarter."

The Female Benevolent Society is only one of the many philanthropic organizations now active in Canada. Like the temperance societies, it believes not only in improving people's lives but also in improving the people themselves. During 1841 members of the Female Benevolent Society of Kingston have been collecting funds and purchasing sewing and knitting materials for distribution to the unemployed and to fatherless families. The finished products are to be given to the poor or sold at the annual bazaar. By "giving out work to employ the poor," according to Harriet Dobbs Cartwright, "industry [will be directed] into the right channels." Advice is handed out with the materials, along with warnings about the "evil of strong drink." Also active are a number of benevolent societies concerned primarily with the welfare of their own members. These include the Foresters, Trinity House, and the Friendly Society. Members make regular contributions and, in times of illness or death, they, their wives, and children receive financial aid from the organization. The growth and diffusion of these societies may be a reflection of a way of life that is becoming more secular, but the churches, especially the Roman Catholic, are still very much involved with the needs of the sick and the poor.

Doctors generally provide their services free to the poor and so are dependent on the more affluent for their fees. The latter may be cared for in the comfort of their homes but the treatment is seldom pleasant. Doctors continue to believe in large doses of medicine and in the efficacy of purges and leeches. Happily, for less acute ailments and for the preservation of health in general, any of a number of pleasant diversions might be prescribed which are beyond the reach of ordinary folk. In summer a picnic excursion into the fresh air of the country on horseback or by carriage might be advised; in winter a similar outing in a sleigh, bundled up in furs, might be recommended. Frequent steamer sailings also provide many opportunities to experience the curative powers of nature. At Montreal, for instance, it is possible to take a day trip to St John's via the *Princess Victoria* and the Champlain and St Lawrence Railway. For those with greater means and more leisure, the doctor might recommend that the patient join a fashionable tour along the waterways stretching between Niagara Falls and Quebec. The sublime scenery of the St Lawrence and the Ottawa would raise the spirits, the numerous military bands in the towns and cities along the way would cheer the mind, and the superior air at Niagara Falls would strengthen the constitution.

For the restoration of health, the Canadian tour has lacked an important ingredient present in the European and even in the American tour – watering-places where respectable society might find pure air, medicinal water, and good cheer. There is no Bath, no Cheltenham, no Karlsbad. There are, however, proposals for turning a site next to the falls at Niagara into a spa. Just north of the Table Rock, hot, cold, and shower baths are to be erected. Over these will be a pump-room, reading-rooms, a library, and refreshment rooms – complete with orchestra. Nearby on Bath Island new bathing houses have been erected at a sulphur spring. The principal attraction of a spa at Niagara will be its cheapness. Half-pay officers and other respectable families of limited means, who cannot think of going to Europe, will be able to set up residence here and meet members of the best society, without the expense of having to entertain them.

Much more modest and certainly less fashionable are the new St Paul Street Baths in Quebec, which offer not only hot and cold baths but also salt water from the sea carried to Quebec by the steamer *Unicorn* on its regular run from Nova Scotia. Just outside the walls of the Upper Town, in the St Johns suburb, is another spa where ladies and gentlemen can take the mineral waters from a recently refurbished spring.

By far the most ambitious Canadian spa is Caledonia Springs, a future rival to Saratoga Springs in New York State. It is situated in the bush about eight miles inland from the Ottawa at L'Orignal and takes its name from the township in Upper Canada in which it is found. The springs were long known to the Indians but, according to its chauvinistic proprietors, "the first intelligent person" to notice them was the Hon. Alexander Grant in about 1806. Later they came to the attention of a man named Kellogg, who realized that wealth awaited the individual who had "sufficient means and energy to make them accessible to invalids. Unfortunately for himself he inherited neither of these qualities." Consequently, little development took place until 1837, when the present proprietors founded the Caledonia Springs Company with a capital of £50,000. A village in the European manner was immediately laid out. At its centre, in Richmond Square, are the springs, hotels, and public buildings. Around the square, building lots have been set aside for the temporary residences of gentlemen's families during the watering season. There are also plans for a "respectable boarding school" that will be hailed with delight, "particularly by those parents whose offspring are suffering from the lassitude and debility inseparable from confined air, and an absence of wholesome exercise." By 1839 a ball-alley was in use and a racket-court and pleasure railroad were being contemplated "in order that visitors, may not be without the amusements and exercise so essential in the pursuit and preservation of health." In 1841 a new and larger hotel opened, replacing one which had burned. It promises good dinners, delicious wines, and obliging attendance. Unhappily for the proprietors, such is "the voracity of the patients, after having taken the Waters for three or four days" that there is "some little difficulty and expense entailed in satisfying their appetites."

There are three springs at the Caledonia spa. They are very close together, yet differ greatly in their qualities and effects. There is a saline spring which acts as an aperient, a white sulphur spring which has the effect of an astringent, and a spring whose water emits gas. There are proposals for using the gas to light the hotel.

The proprietors attribute almost miraculous cures to the waters – especially in cases of rheumatism, diseases of the liver, dropsy, dyspepsia, scrofula, fever and ague, and jaundice. "Almost superhuman" cures are effected in cases of syphilis. Mercury, commonly used in treating syphilis and other disorders, often produces stubborn – even fatal – complaints in those treated. These are "invariably eradicated" at Caledonia Springs.

Caledonia Springs can be reached in one day by passenger steamer from Montreal. Plans for a stage – possibly already in effect – between Cornwall and L'Orignal will enable both the invalid and the fashionable tourist travelling the St Lawrence route to make a pleasant diversion to the springs. The growing reputation of the spa's waters is attracting visitors of the "highest respectability" from every part of the British provinces, from the remote sections of the United States, and even from the West Indies. Whatever the efficacy of the cure, taking the waters at a spa in the woods is certainly far more agreeable than treatment in a cheerless hospital in town. Perhaps that is how it is meant to be: spas for the rich, hospitals for the poor.

Visitors to Caledonia Springs are not lured by its location in the wilds. On the contrary, every effort is being made to assure them that the "improvements of civilization" have been imposed on "wild and undressed nature." Ladies now promenade where once the bear and wolf had prowled; the sun may be seen rising in the east and setting in the west where formerly the dark, impervious forest had sullenly stood; and even the woodpecker's loud tap has given way to the gentle click of the composing stick. Nature might truly aid in restoring the care-worn man of business to health, but it is not to be the nature of the raw wilderness of the Canadian bush but rather the tamed nature of a half-remembered Bath, Brighton, or Edinburgh New Town.

Near Caledonia Springs is a fine lake filled with bass where visitors are invited to fish – or rather where *male* visitors are invited to fish. Custom excludes females from this and similar cheerful and healthy outdoor activities such as "shooting," hunting, and boating. Even the poorest male immigrant, hacking a living from the bush, may indulge in these "sports" reserved for the wealthy few in the old country, but they are not accessible to his wife. She is expected to occupy herself close to home, often performing tasks considered servile back in Britain. When "cabin fever" sets in, the man can always escape outside and chop away at the trees. It is unlikely that tearing up clothing for making mats offers a comparable release for his wife. Her very existence is consumed by her house and family

Native hunting techniques were sometimes copied, including fishing from canoes at night with the aid of birchbark torches. Novices did not always allow for the refraction of light by the water and sometimes ended up among the fish when they jabbed with their spears in the wrong spot while standing in the bow of the canoe. Large numbers of fish were taken in this way, but perhaps as many more were merely wounded and left in agony to die.

Fishing party on Lake Charles by J.P. Cockburn. Watercolour, National Gallery of Canada

SHOOTING AND FISHING

"Shooting" and fishing provided a delightful diversion for officers and gentlemen of the towns, notably for those who had come from a society where such pleasures were reserved for the landed few. For those who had grown up in Canada where there were no game laws and where anyone could go hunting or fishing, these activities had lost much of their social cachet, particularly in the countryside where they were a mundane part of daily existence life for even the humblest of Canadians.

Nature provided Canada with vast amounts of game. Salmon, trout, bass, and pike were taken in prodigious quantities and were important in the maintenance of the immigrant family. So, too, were deer, moose, and birds such as the wild turkey and the passenger pigeon.

The large and beautiful passenger pigeon – it was seventeen inches long, blue-grey with a rich wine breast – made for good eating and seemed to be inexhaustible in numbers. The American naturalist John J. Audubon estimated that one flock of these birds, one mile wide and taking three hours to pass, contained more than 1,115,136,000 birds. Because they flew so close to one another and so near the ground, they were not difficult to take. Indeed, the young birds (known by their short tails) could easily be knocked down with long poles. Nets were also used, often with decoys or stool pigeons to lure the birds into them.

and, by the time she is thirty, signs of old age begin to appear. After seven years in the bush, Susanna Moodie said she looked double her age. "I clung to my solitude," she wrote, "I did not like to be dragged from it to mingle in gay scenes, in a busy town, and with gaily-dressed people. I was no longer fit for the world; I had lost all relish for the pursuits and pleasures which are so essential to its votaries; I was contented to live and die in obscurity." Simple conversation with strangers becomes difficult and travellers depart with unflattering impressions of sallow complexions (caused by overheated houses?) and faces dejected and emaciated. Unlike their sisters left behind in old world, women in Canada seldom work outside the house and spend most of their lives within the confines of its walls. Like a bird in a cage, they might flutter for a while but in time they become too timid to take wing – even when it is possible to do so.

In November 1841 the Toronto *Patriot* published from the *Musical World* an endorsement by Dr Rush* of the value of singing as a palliative for young ladies debarred by social custom from other kinds of healthy exercise. Besides soothing the cares of domestic life, singing exercises the "organs of the breast" and helps prevent those diseases to which the climate and other causes exposed them. Consumption, he said, was rare among singers and he did not know of "more than one case of spitting blood amongst them."

Calomel, a preparation of mercury, is one of the common cure-alls for most disorders. It is sometimes given in amounts large enough to cause poisoning. (A poisoning which is said to respond to the waters of Caledonia Springs.) Calomel is used for a variety of purposes including purging – even for a disease like cholera which, in itself, produces a massive purging of its victims. Dr Elam Stimson of London, Upper Canada, was among the physicians who treated their patients with large doses of calomel during the 1832 cholera

---

* The Dr Rush referred to by the *Musical World* was undoubtedly the celebrated Benjamin Rush, a signer of the American Constitution and a well-respected physician whose ideas still had currency the 1840s. He had great faith in bleeding – sometimes to the point where the patient fainted. Apparently Dr Rush believed that the body contained twice as much blood as it actually did. The blood was caught in a bowl and used to diagnose the patient's condition by making observations on the changes which occurred during the hours following its being taken. Such bleeding was done with a lancet. "Lively medical leeches" were also used and jars filled with them could be found in pharmacies and doctors' offices. Treatment might call for a single leech on an eyelid or a hundred on the abdomen.

epidemic. He also prescribed ginger tea and alcohol and, of course, copious bleeding. Many of his patients died, including his wife and son. (Soon after his wife's death, he married her younger sister and settled in St George, where he is still practising.)

Doctors continue to believe in massive intervention and no matter how unpleasant the treatment, the patient at least has the assurance that something is being done. Yet many people turn to quacks – especially for chronic or social diseases. Advertisements abound with cures for cancer, rheumatism, dyspepsia, and the like as well as for ailments the victims wish to keep concealed. Doubtless there have been many responses to the blandishments of the Albany Lock Hospital: "country patients residing at a distance – and all other patients who prefer writing instead of a personal interview – can be treated with equal success on describing minutely their case by letter, and enclosing a remittance for advice and medicine ... medicines will be securely packed, carefully protected from observation, and sent without delay to the place appointed."

GOITRE

Goitre, particularly in Upper Canada, may have been responsible for much of the diminished vigour, mental sluggishness, and depressed spirits experienced by women like Susanna Moodie. Goitre is an ailment caused by a deficiency of iodine in the diet. It was found most often in places removed from the sea and where recent glaciation had occurred. In these areas neither the soil nor the water contained adequate traces of iodine. As in many disorders involving deficiencies, women were more frequently affected than men simply because they bore children. In 1841 the cause of goitre was unknown but that it was largely restricted to specific regions was generally recognized. Indeed, in England it was often referred to as "Derbyshire Neck" from its common occurrence in this inland county, and it was well known that a cure could be effected simply by moving to another area.

The waters of Caledonia Springs did contain iodine, but a prolonged stay would have been necessary to decrease the goitre symptoms. This may be why no miracles were claimed for this disease – although oversight was a much more likely reason for its omission from the list of cures.

DEATH OF
LORD SYDENHAM

When Lord Sydenham arrived in Kingston in May 1841,
his arm was in a sling – his gout was acting up. This
chronic ailment of the joints was more common in the nineteenth century than it is today and was largely confined to
males. Why this was so is not clear; the exact cause of the
disorder remains uncertain, although heredity is a factor.
Attacks of gout came without warning to those who were
predisposed. These could be triggered by dampness, chills,
overtiredness, and, especially, by diet. Lord Sydenham,
a man of driving ambition, had pushed himself very hard
in Canada and, by July 1841, he was so tired that he had
sent off his resignation, hoping to return to England
by September in order to recuperate. To get a feeling for
the troubled colony he was governing, frequent dinner
parties were held. He liked rich food, porter, and cham-
pagne – all designed to bring on attacks. When he was able,
Sydenham took daily exercise on foot in the grounds of
Government House or further afield on horseback. It was
during one of these outings in early September that his
horse tripped, throwing His Lordship from the saddle and
breaking his right leg. He also suffered a deep cut above
the knee, which was filled with gravel from being dragged
along the newly macadamized road. The accident occurred
between the Kingston Hospital and Government House.
Even had the hospital been in operation, there would have
been no question of taking him there. The nearby work-
men who came to his rescue immediately carried him
home. In a few days tetanus developed from the wound,
possibly because of manure on the road, and on 19 September the governor general was dead – killed by a disease
much more prevalent among farmers, workers, and others
subject to traumatic injuries than among members of
respectable society.

In early August a Dr Williams took up residence at Mrs E. Lane's private boarding house in the Upper Town of Quebec. Before offering his services to suffering humanity, he submitted documents concerning his past to the mayor for inspection. Now nearing seventy, he had practised for many years in London, France, the Netherlands, and the United States, and had been appointed honorary oculist to their late majesties Louis XVIII and Charles X. At present he held the same appointment with King Louis-Philippe of France and King Leopold of Belgium. Dr Williams was especially anxious to serve the unfortunate of Quebec and urged the rich to send him their poor to be treated. The mayor could not accede to the good doctor's request that his arrival be announced with placards under his worship's patronage but he did offer his assistance in bringing Williams's reputation to the public's attention.

No one questioned why this distinguished, elderly doctor who had walked with kings should have taken up residence at Mrs Lane's boarding house in this remote corner of the empire. Instead, persons with "weakness of sight" or "inflammation of the eyes" made their way to his door where – for $3 – they were supplied with a packet containing remedies 1, 2, 3, 4, 5, and 9 and a copy of Williams's book, *Every Man His Own Oculist*. Blind persons living some distance away needed only to describe their cases in a letter (enclosing the customary fee in advance) and send it post-paid to Dr Williams. Each day at noon Dr Williams made public a display of his philanthropic nature by receiving the poor in the schoolroom of the Methodist church.

From Quebec Williams went on to Montreal, where he again treated the poor in the Methodist church. The mayor, Peter McGill, was present at one session and was so favourably impressed by what he saw that he publicly urged Dr Williams to remain longer in the city. The doctor graciously consented to do so.

After finally gathering up his packets, Williams left Montreal and headed along the St Lawrence into Upper Canada. Meanwhile, so that no one would be missed, Mr Williams Jr, his grandson, carried the remedies to the villages and towns along the Ottawa route, and later joined up with his grandfather at Kingston. By keeping on the move, Williams was able to maintain his philanthropic reputation until he was well into western Canada. Eventually, his past caught up with him from the United States, where he had been treating the afflicted before coming to Canada. Words like "quack," "humbug," and "imposter" were hurled about and, at the moment, Williams is being bound over on three different counts and is waiting to appear at the next quarter session.

Age brings with it deteriorating sight and decaying teeth. Opticians and spectacle makers like Mr Prince, Palace Street, Quebec, stock eye-glasses of a quality "rarely obtained out of Europe." Since spectacles are frequently considered a mark of intelligence, they are worn with pride – often conspicuously – with mountings, carefully selected, of gold, silver, tortoise shell, pearl, steel, or horn. False teeth are another matter. Here the object is to "supply any deficiency of the mouth and gums, so completely as to prevent the possibility of detection." Dr Jones of Kingston is able to do this because he possesses the secret of "making Incorruptible Porcelain Teeth." His colleague, Dr Goldey, prefers mineral teeth, which he inserts on "the unerring principle of atmosphere pressure." Decayed teeth are often stuffed – a technique used for many years – but extraction, the ultimate dental procedure, is frequently resorted to and mouths with missing teeth contribute much to the ill-health of their owners.

Whether it is doctors, eye-glasses, teeth, or patent medicines, people are reassured by being told that the object in question is from Europe or the United States and that it has been employed by the rich and powerful. Even the promoters of *Roach and Bed Bug Bane* assure their customers that their product is regularly used by "the most wealthy and fashionable ladies in Chestnut-street, Philadelphia." People are easily captivated by the word "scientific." If something is both scientific and exotic – *and* supported by respectable members of society – it can hardly fail. Such has been the acceptance of phrenology.

LONG HAIR BECOMING FASHIONABLE

Phrenological examinations of young men were becoming more difficult now that they were wearing their hair long and growing beards. Fine faces and noble foreheads were fast disappearing from view, much to the disgust of the Kingston *Chronicle and Gazette*, which quoted an old and experienced hairdresser who predicted that baldness would be the end result of the fashion. Meanwhile, it claimed that the youths would be mortified by being assimilated to goats, baboons, and orangutans. Of course, this was not the first time long hair was fashionable; during the 1830s John Bigsby was surprised to find pigtails lingering on among the old men of Lower Canada, "among other relicts of the days of Louis XV."

Phrenology originated in Vienna at the beginning of the present century and has been all the rage in Great Britain during the past decade. Now it has spread to the Canadas. By studying the development of the skull, the phrenologist is able to appraise the mental capacity, peculiar talents, and disposition of his subject. A Mr Fletcher presented lectures in phrenology every evening at the Quebec Mechanics' Institute during August. (The connection with the institute lent support to the scientific validity of the talks in the same way that Dr Williams's choice of the Methodist church implied the philanthropic nature of his practice.) In the mornings Mr Fletcher was available for examinations and for providing written descriptions of character. Through his science, he could accurately point out those feelings that should be restrained and those that needed encouragement. By means of his chart, which was a perfect "mirror of nature," the mind is able to "view itself, to judge of the actuating motive of every action, and to guide itself in the true path to prosperity, happiness and virtue." Some parents are persuaded that phrenology is of immense importance; through it they may learn in which occupation or profession their children would be most likely to excel.

Once having chosen a suitable occupation or profession for the child, it is no easy matter to have him suitably educated in this country. Partly as a result of the events leading up to the union, the school system in both Canadas is still in chaos. However, there is reason to believe that the situation will soon improve. One of the first acts of the new government sitting in Kingston was the Common Schools Act, which is intended to replace much of the haphazard schooling in both Canadas with a unified system. Because of the diverse nature of the population, a "principle of dissent" is included. It provides that "any number of persons of a different faith from the majority" in any "township or parish" might notify the school commission of their intention to withdraw from the control of that body, choose their own trustees, and "establish and maintain one or more common schools" for the minority. Such schools would be eligible for government support. The principle should satisfy the English-speaking residents of Lower Canada who fear domination by the French-speaking Catholic majority.*

---

* Later the principle of dissent would become the cornerstone of the separate school systems in Ontario and Quebec. Thus, perhaps unintentionally, both English and French culture would be saved from assimilation through an educational system separated on the basis of religion rather than language.

THE NEED FOR
CANADIAN SCHOOL BOOKS

In the preface to his *Canada Spelling Book,* Alexander David-
son drew attention to the crying need for a speller suitable
for Canadian use. "At the present time ... those of United
States' origin are the most numerous. While Spelling
Books from England are to *us* necessarily defective, not
being suited to our scenery and other localities, those of a
foreign origin are liable to more serious objections."

The Rev. A.N. Bethune of Cobourg, editor of *The Church,*
found in the *Canadian Spelling Book* "a very positive incul-
cation of the duty of loyalty, and of that great obligation
upon which loyalty and every other sound principle is
founded – religion – is diffused throughout the work; so
that the good subject and the conscientious Christian, may
safely place it in the hands of his children. On these
grounds, and from its general simplicity and cheapness I
cannot but express an strong hope that it will entirely supersede the questionable work, Webster's Spelling Book." The
Rev. R. McGill of Niagara was in agreement and would
have been happy to see the *Canadian Spelling Book* replace
those "adapted to political institutions different from ours."

In 1841 an edition of Walker's Dictionary was published
by Messrs Armour & Ramsay of Montreal and was wel-
comed by the *Montreal Transcript,* which trusted that
it would "supersede the editions from the States ... containing a very partial and incorrect account of the late war [of
1812]." The dictionary contained an appendix of Ameri-
canisms to "assist the scholar in detecting the words in
common use in the United States of America, and not un-
frequently heard in the British American Provinces; but
which stand upon no adequate authority, and are not to be
met with in the best English authors."

English-speaking Canada is becoming increasingly fertile ground for new ideas in education – especially if they originate abroad. English influence can be seen in the stress on the classics in the elitist grammar schools of Upper Canada. Among these, Toronto's Upper Canada College is the best known. Irish experience pervades much of the public school system of Upper Canada. Yet the Scottish influence can also be felt in the more democratic approach to education and in the greater emphasis on the sciences. From the United States has come the new office of Superintendent of Education to administer the Common Schools Act. From that country also has come a number of textbooks – to the discomfort of many in authority who view them as sources of "the poison of disaffection." To build a more loyal population, the British influence must be strengthened. Education is being promoted in the press and by members of the upper classes. Both see ignorance as a threat to peace and the social order. On a more abstract level there is talk of the importance of education in creating the "moral man." Other discussion is more utilitarian and focuses on the need for greater education among farmers, so that they might be instructed in better farming techniques. It is argued that more education would raise the status of farming. This may be so, but in 1841 there were already complaints that education is causing farmers to drift from the land and that they and other manual workers are becoming ashamed of using their hands.

French-Canadian education is largely cut off from outside influences and to a large extent has resisted contamination from an alien religion and language. At the time of the Conquest it had compared favourably with most European countries, but during the two generations of disruption that followed, the level of education declined sharply – especially among the male population. By the 1820s so few men could read or write that an 1827 petition to the government of Lower Canada carried 87,000 signatures of which 78,000 were signed with a cross. Yet it was possible to receive an excellent education in French in Canada in several institutions provided by the Roman Catholic church. The two oldest and best known are in Quebec – the Ursuline Convent (1639) and the Quebec Seminary (1663).

The Ursuline Convent is housed in a plain stone building in the Upper Town that was built a century and a half ago. At present it contains about forty nuns, a lady superior, and a few novitiates. Here, as in other religious establishments in Quebec and Montreal, there has been difficulty in keeping up the numbers. Now and then a candidate for admission will come out from France, but few Canadians females seem willing to undergo the labour and to submit

Those wishing to combine a study of educational attainment and national differences had only to go to Niagara Falls, where "every wall, and tree, and door, and window, in the

vicinity, was covered with initials, and names, and dates, and details, and eulogies, as contributions from the innumerable visitors. Lines, distiches, paragraphs, pages and volumes of trash – in prose and verse, and all the thousand gradations of doggerel, [were] diamonded upon panes, and pencilled upon window frames and doors, and hacked and hewed into the walls and benches and trees; both on the British and American side, so as to overwhelm the whole neighbourhood." (The pavilion was later destroyed by fire "and thus half a million of commemorative aspirations after wooden celebrity and immortality, [were] swept into oblivion by the ruthless flames.") "There was a difference observable in these incriptions, illustrative, perhaps, of some distinguishing traits of national character ... English visitors [were] generally content with leaving their initials, date and address; whereas the Americans far more frequently appended some expression of feeling – original or in a quotation. The French, Germans and Italians were unmerciful in their admiration, and sad monopolizers of space. Some of the couplets and verses were respectable enough; but all the writers appear to sink under the magnitude of their theme. The majority of the original effusions, however, were the most utterly abominable trash ...

"Never were any poor trees so barbarously treasted as those in Goat Island. They [were] carved and cut all over with tens of thousands of names ... one gentleman's appelation [was] thrity feet up the stem of a very large maple, where there were no branches to hold by, and which was too big to be embraced: he must therefore have brought a ladder half a mile to climb to immortality. The name of this aspiring hero [was] *Phinehas James*, of Philadelphia, and the date of his elevation, 10th June 1830."

W. Henry, *Trifles from my Port-folio*, vol. II, 92–95

to the discipline of a religious vocation. The main work of the convent is the education of girls from the Quebec area. It is said that over three-quarters of the young ladies of Quebec have received instruction there. Under the present regime, as under the French, the Ursulines have been closely associated with the official ruling class and, from the time of the conquest when they nursed the wounded British soldiers (and knitted long woolen stockings for the Highland troops), they have contributed much to bettering relations between the two peoples.

Like the Ursuline Convent, the Quebec Seminary has also received many English and Protestant students. Founded by Bishop Laval in 1663, the seminary was intended to educate young men for the priesthood only, but when the Jesuit Order – which had taken charge of the general education of the children of the community – was dissolved by a decree of the French king in 1764, the directors of the seminary opened their institution to any who wished to attend. No charge (other than for lights and fuel) is made for day-pupils, while boarders pay only for their maintenance. During 1841 there were approximately 150 day-pupils and 150 boarders. They follow a curriculum consisting of Greek, Latin, mathematics, history, belles-lettres, astronomy, chemistry, mineralogy, and natural philosophy. Most students attend the seminary from five to seven years, although some remain for nine years. It is said by those who attend the annual exhibition at the end of each college year that few colleges in Europe could produce a greater number of well-educated youths. Apparently this opinion is not completely unanimous: one British officer has complained about the "specimens of young British colonists" he sees emerging from the seminaries of Lower Canada. He feels that the mode of teaching adopted by the brothers is not well calculated "to expand the closed bud of genius." The library of the Quebec Seminary contains 8000 volumes, with "valuable philosophical apparatus" and an interesting cabinet of Indian antiquities, minerals, fossils, and curiosities. Besides the seminary and the convent, there are a number of minor French schools in Quebec, including one in the suburb of St Roch where Antoine Légaré is a teacher. He has gone further in his classical studies than any layman in the country. At a time and place where the lay teacher is generally regarded as a person who has failed in another occupation or is merely marking time until something better comes along, Légaré is exceptional in dedicating his life to teaching. It is more common to find that this year's teacher was last year's tavern keeper and next year's wharfinger. Educated women in reduced circumstances sometimes resort to teaching. One of these is the heroine of the late war with the United States, Laura Secord. She was widowed

PRIVATE SCHOOLS IN QUEBEC

Private schools were mostly one-man or one-woman affairs
that came and went as the fortunes of the teachers rose or
fell. Advertisements for them appeared in the newspapers of
Quebec and throughout the Canadas. Typical was Mr Hennessy's announcement in 1841 of his intention to "com-
mence his usual method of teaching a select number of boys"
on the first of May. His school was in the lower part of
Mr Hattigan's house in the lower part of Mountain Street.
In support of his qualifications, Mr Hennessy felt that it
was sufficient to inform his friends and those whom it may
concern that he still knows how to demonstrate Newton's
Binomial and to illustrate Cardan's theorem, and that he
shall never forget the old rule of

x the years and y the months explain,
Hence by a quadratic you my age may gain, &c.

More fashionably situated were the new schools of Mr Jenkins for boys and Mrs Jenkins for girls at 11 Fabrique Street.
Mrs Jenkins's seminary for young ladies was designed "to
give only a plain, useful education." The course of instruction was to include reading, writing, arithmetic, plain
needlework, English grammar, history, and geography. Her
advertisement in the *Quebec Mercury* stressed that "without
any intention to depreciate those ornamental requirements,
which form so large a portion of modern female education
Mrs J. trusts that all prudent parents and guardians must be
convinced, that the ornamental superstructure should always
be proportioned to the foundation of solid information
which should form its support." Readers must, however,
have had a nagging suspicion that the curriculum was based
not so much on Mrs Jenkins's philosophy of education as
upon her own limited attainments, for arithmetic and writing were to be taught by Mr Jenkins "without interfering
in the least with the discharge of his duty to his own pupils";
despite her views on "ornamental acquirements," she was
willing "should sufficient encouragement be given" to
engage the assistance of a lady "eminently qualified to in-
struct in French, ornamental needle-work, &c."

in 1841 and left without financial resources. At sixty-six, she has been forced to opened a school at her Chippawa cottage.

On the English side there is no equivalent of the Ursuline Convent or the Quebec Seminary, although there are a number of Sunday schools attached to the various Protestant denominations. These are well attended and are said to "produce very beneficial results upon the minds of youth." There are also a few infant schools, a Madras School, a National School, a British and Canadian School, a School of the Quebec Education Society, and a charity school for the deaf and dumb. Tuition for children of the poor is free in all of these schools. Nevertheless, the English system is inadequate and many parents have had to resort to private schools. This is particularly galling when the Grammar School of the Royal Institution for the Advancement of Learning is offering no classes, even though its building and master are supported with public funds. It was intended to be a free school.*

As in Lower Canada "there remaineth yet very much land to be possessed" in the field of education in Upper Canada. Progress in education in Upper Canada has been restrained by a long-standing conflict between the Anglican minority, who are determined to hang on to a privileged position in the educational system, and the majority of the population. The struggle is reflected in legislation passed by the provincial government. For example, there was an act in 1807 for the founding of elitist grammar schools similar to English "public" schools and in 1816 there was a Common Schools Act much in the American tradition. In 1838 there were twelve grammar schools for the privileged few, including Upper Canada College, and 651 common schools for the remainder of the population with 14,776 pupils. Probably only half of all school-aged children in this province of 400,000 are attending school, and many of these for only brief periods.

Upper Canada College, Toronto, by T. Young, stone by J.H. Bufford, lithograph by N. Currier. NAC

The typical common school is a one-room log building with an open fireplace. Students sit on backless benches facing the teacher, who sits or stands behind a tall pulpit-like desk. Blackboards or maps are rare and books consist of whatever might be avail-

* Established in 1801, the RIAL represented a largely unsuccessful attempt on the part of the English minority to establish a school system in Lower Canada.

THE LITERARY GARLAND

January 1841 saw the commencement of the third volume
of *The Literary Garland*, a monthly magazine devoted to
the advancement of general literature. Its Montreal
publisher, John Lovell, encouraged "the advancement of
Canadian literature." Among the authors he published
were Susanna Moodie, Catharine Parr Trail, Anna
Jameson, and John Richardson.

Victoria College,
Coburg
by W.H. Bartlett.
In Willis,
Canadian
Scenery, *vol. 2,*
facing p. 52

VICTORIA COLLEGE

The Victoria Academy building near Cobourg, with
its portico and cupola, was very imposing. It had been
erected by subscription among members of the
Methodist persuasion, who were very numerous in
that part of Upper Canada.

able – a Bible, old readers, arithmetic books, and spellers. Much of the teaching is by rote. In the newly settled areas, especially, attendance is sporadic, particularly in the spring and fall when children are needed at home. The result is a boorish society that has elicited unfavourable remarks from the likes of Lord Durham, Susanna Moodie, and Anna Jameson. It has been observed that there are hundreds of taverns but few bookstores in the country. To be fair, many people do read the newspapers and these are often available in the taverns.

The year 1841 ended on a promising note as far as education was concerned: the recently established Victoria Academy near Coburg was soon to be joined by two other institutions of higher learning: Queen's College in the new capital and the Diocesan College of Canada East [later Bishop's University] in Lennoxville in the Eastern Townships. Lennoxville was chosen for the new college because "it is in the centre of a rich agricultural district, easily accessible from all parts of the province, among an orderly and quiet population." Although the professors in the college (and teachers at an associated grammar school) are to be clergy of the Church of England "and graduates of some University of Reputation in the British Dominions," students of other persuasions are to be admitted to both institutions. It is intended that English-speaking students should no longer be forced to gain a college education either through attending one of the French seminaries in Lower Canada or by going abroad to some institution of higher education in the United States or Great Britain. However, since the college prospectus calls for only a Principal and "at least one other Professor," it is doubtful if it can supply the place of New England colleges or British universities.

In December it was learned that the Rev. Mr Liddell of Edinburgh's Lady Glenorchy's Church had been appointed as principal of Queen's College in Kingston and it was expected that he would be on the 3 December sailing of the steam packet bound for Halifax. It was hoped by the Kingston *Chronicle and Gazette* "that the institution would now go speedily into operation."

In education, medicine, law, and in other areas as well, the spirit of improvement was continuing to grow in the Canadas of 1841. It was most apparent in the larger centres but its beneficial effects were beginning to be felt throughout the country – although not as strongly as some might have wished.

Chapter V

Diversions

Robertson was bemused by the affectations of Quebec society. In his more guarded moments he would refer to it as "piano in the parlour, porridge in the kitchen." He often said that the true measure of a people was the manner in which they took their leisure, and this is the subject of his final chapter. All in all, in Quebec he felt that the pretensions of good taste and civilization were not always reflected in practice.

Visiting "artistes" took advantage of Quebec's remoteness and naïveté and, in their handbills, often associated themselves with major cities or with the royal courts of Europe. British performers, sometimes well past their prime, attempted to extend their careers by heading to the colonies, where audiences might be less sophisticated.

Although hardly a religious man himself, Robertson could not help but be aware that religion was much more the fashion in the Edinburgh of recent years than it had been in his youth. With its rise had come a number of sects and increasing competition. In Quebec he witnessed a renewal in the Roman Catholic church and was intrigued by newspaper accounts of Protestant camp meetings in Upper Canada. Like the "bees" that also fascinated him, they were part of the levelling system.

Much of Quebec society centred on the garrison. This was no longer as true in Edinburgh as it had been two or three decades ago during the French Revolution and the "Bonaparte wars" when the city was filled with troops. In Quebec the officers were responsible for some of the best winter assemblies, although they could hardly measure up to those held in assembly rooms in Edinburgh's George Street. Robertson went along to many of these with his son and daughter-in-law. Because of his knee, he was forced to sit on the sidelines, where he watched in amusement.

Robertson had always loved skating and curling and was a life-long member of the Duddingston Curling Society. (It was in curling that he first injured his knee.) From his description of curling in Canada, it is obvious that he envied Canadian Scots their long sunny winters with many weeks of the sport.

In Edinburgh Robertson frequently attended meetings of the Speculative Society, and so it was natural that he would become active in the Literary and Historical Society of Quebec. Once again he was to discover that pretensions did not quite measure up to performance. Nevertheless, Robertson's social life was rich in Quebec and he had little difficulty in filling his days. At the end of the chapter there is a sense of relief that he did not end up in Toronto where, apart from taverns and low drinking-houses, the only place of assembly and amusement was the commercial newsroom.

*T*wo forces were in tension in the Canadian society of 1841: one pulling in the direction of improvement and refinement; the other towards Philistinism, provincialism, and rowdyism. All too frequently the latter force exerted the stronger pull, as when Il Diavolo Antonio and his celebrated family "exhibited the science of gymnastics" in Quebec late in the summer of 1841. According to the *Mercury* they did not receive the patronage they deserved from a public that lately "had flocked in crowds to witness entertainments of a far inferior character." Except for the police in attendance, there had been all too few spectators to witness the fine performance of the three young Diavolos in the comic Chinese Dance of the Tea Pickers or *Ballet des Chinois, Pas de Trois*.

What were these inferior entertainments the *Mercury* had in mind? Was it the double-jointed 330-pound, seven foot three inch American youth of twenty, billed as "the largest, best proportioned and strongest human in the world" who could be seen for a shilling and threepence a head? Or was it the visit of the only camelopard [giraffe] in North America? As with the double-jointed giant, the drawing power of the exhibit had depended upon its being hidden from sight as it travelled from place to place. How this had been accomplished on the roads and steamers is not clear. The camelopard's schedule was tight and he could remain in Quebec for only a few days, since he must "cross the Atlantic before the weather becomes too cold for this native of burning climes." On his way south he was shown in Montreal in the Old Tattersall Court in St James Street, where "the strictest decorum" was "enforced to render the exhibition a place of rational amusement and fashionable retreat." From

Montreal he had resumed his southward journey, but never again was he to experience his burning clime. A few days after leaving the city, he breathed his last at St John's, Lower Canada.

Giraffes and giants are difficult enough to keep hidden, but pity the poor Quebecker who suffered a considerable loss when he put on a display of fireworks that were enjoyed (without the payment of admission) throughout his neighbourhood, in spite of the unfortunate choice of a night when the moon was full. Quite the opposite was true of the circuses, which often intentionally displayed their best in parades knowing that the public would then be willing to pay for what it hoped would be even better.

Possibly the *Mercury* had in mind the circus of S.B. Howes, Mabie & Co, which had been in Quebec only a few days before Il Diavolo Antonio's stay. With upwards of eighty men and horses, it was billed as "the largest circus in the world." The circus parade was led by a band playing popular airs of the day. The musicians were the most talented that could be procured, "Italian, English and Americans, without any regard to prejudice of nations, having been hired at enormous salaries for the purpose of securing the very best performers." Following the band were mounted equestrians and a train of elegant baggage wagons. Or perhaps the *Mercury* had been thinking of yet another equestrian circus that had been in town just before the arrival of the Howes, Mabie circus.

Most of the circuses and other diversions involving performers from out of town are squeezed into a few hectic weeks during the late summer and early fall. The evenings are still long enough to encourage people to go out, yet cool enough to make the theatres bearable – certainly more bearable than theatres further south in the sweltering home towns of many of the entertainers. European artists also arrive at this time year, taking advantage of the favourable travelling conditions. Roads are as good as they are ever likely to be and the steamers are much less crowded now that most of the immigrants have gone up-country.

With so much to see and hear, Canadians are frequently faced with tantalizing choices, especially when the choice is between the titillating and the uplifting. Many entertainers are aware of this problem and present a wide variety of offerings on different evenings in order to appeal to the broadest public possible. Potential audiences are small and it is often necessary to draw on the same people a number of times. That is why John Braham, the great English tenor, gave concerts both sacred and profane in Montreal during August 1841. He is now in his late sixties and past his prime – a fact that reminded his audiences of the old adage "that time changes, and that we, alas, change with it."

Braham was unfortunate enough to have his tour coincide with that of the spirited young *prima donna,* Euphrasia Borghese, who captivated her audiences with the brilliance and excitement of her Italian style. Yet even Mlle Borghese was careful not to bore her listeners and she shared her platform with Etienne Voizel, "Tenor of the Private Music of the King of France," Henry Billet, "First Violin cellist of the Private Music of the Emperor of Russia," and – as if that were not enough – the Band of the 7th Hussars. The theatre season of 1841 came to a close with several performances by two of the most celebrated actors of the English stage, Fanny Fitzwilliam and John Buckstone. Both are irrepressible comedians. "Such mirth was never excited in the Montreal Theatre," said the *Morning Courier,* "and is not likely to be again when the four nights engagement of Mrs Fitzwilliam and Mr Buckstone are concluded."

JOHN BRAHAM (c1774–1856)

Born in London of German Jewish parents, Braham was orphaned at an early age and for a time sold pencils in the street. His musical talent was recognized before puberty and by his mid-twenties Braham was singing in the leading opera houses of Italy. Through his music, he accumulated a large fortune. This was lost in the 1830s as a result of unwise investments and he was forced to return to the stage. By then his voice had suffered the ravages of time. In 1840 he went to America with his son for a tour that eventually took him to Canada in 1841. Braham possessed a prodigious talent and could sing with utmost perfection, but he preferred to appeal to the baser instincts of his audiences by using vulgar and tricky displays and sensational effects.
By 1841 his powers had diminished to the point where this was not enough to satisfy even his unsophisticated Canadian listeners. The tour was not a success.

For those who shun the frivolous, there is a dawning awareness that nature can provide amusement of a "useful" and "instructive" character that is highly beneficial, especially to the young. Natural history is becoming ever more popular and exponents of its various branches are travelling up and down the land. Of course, some are

THE VIOLONCELLO

Canadians accustomed to the fiddle were very much taken by the 'cello performances of Henry Billet. They found it difficult to conceive how it was possible for an individual to accomplish more upon the violin either as respected "fineness of tone or rapidity of execution." So enthusiastic was the audience with the manner in which M. Billet handled his "unwieldy instrument" that it frequently broke into applause in the middle of a piece.

JOHN BALDWIN BUCKSTONE
(1802–1879) AND
FANNY ELIZABETH FITZWILLIAM
(1801–1854)

John Baldwin Buckstone and Fanny Elizabeth Fitzwilliam were at the height of their powers when they visited Canada in 1841 as part of a lengthy North American tour that took them as far afield as New Orleans and Havana. Buckstone's unusual appearance, distinctive voice, and infectious geniality enabled him to get away with a type of humour that might have been considered too broad if attempted by a more ordinary actor. Fanny Fitzwilliam was on her second visit to America, where it had been predicted she would make more money in the United States than any actress except Fanny Kemble, another English visitor. Her acting had much sweetness and womanliness and she was said to be unequalled in the portrayal of country girls, Irish peasants, and the like. She was also an excellent singer. She and Buckstone were to be married late in 1854, but on 11 November she was seized with cholera and within a few hours was dead.

CAMP MEETING

Although its origin could be traced back to England, the Methodist camp meeting was very much a creation of the New World. It evolved on the western frontier of the United States and then spread to the lower Great Lakes before crossing into Canada, where it found fertile ground in the back country. During the early years of settlement there were usually too few people to support a place of public worship and the settlers learned to make do without one. In time they grew lax in their religious observances and often sank into stupid apathy or contented indifference. Meanwhile, life in the new land bred a spirit of equality and independence that greatly weakened the desire to return to the authority and discipline of the church as they had known it. The rigid class structure of denominations like the Church of England, where rented pews kept people in their proper places, no longer held much popular appeal.

At the camp meeting everyone was equal and the only authority was the Spirit – even It worked privately within each individual. Those receiving the Spirit often fell, writhing and shrieking, to the ground. Youths, both male and female, appeared to be especially receptive to the Spirit and rolled about with unbridled enthusiasm. Above the din the preacher thundered on, convinced that the greater the tumult, the more successful was the discourse; and the people became accustomed to view their moans and lamentations as true signs of their own gracious condition. This was the American Gospel, and in Canada it created tensions with the more staid traditions of Great Britain, Ireland, and France. Clergymen in settled churches were not happy with these preachers, who were said to arouse the spirit without impressing the mind. Yet, as if to prove an old Russian proverb that people tended to become like what they opposed, the ministers themselves were driven to adopt the erratic mode of teaching of the itinerant preacher in place of the routine work of the ministry. Critics of camp meetings – and there were many in 1841 – claimed that the Spirit emanated not from the God of Light but from the Prince of Darkness, and that he converted the meetings into carnivals of all the criminal pleasures of a degenerate world, including drunkenness and adultery.

charlatans and mountebanks but others are men of learning. The difference is not always apparent from the handbills: in both cases they are couched in "philosophical" and "scientific" vocabularies. Demonstrations with the aid of scientific instruments are often promised and use was to be made of the magic lantern. Attendance at such talks could be justified on religious grounds by the more sober-minded since they not only bring the listener closer to nature but nearer to nature's God as well. Perhaps the most successful formula for sending an audience away filled with exhilaration was devised by two speakers who visited St Catharines in August. They administered laughing gas following their illustrated lecture on astronomy.

Such effete diversions might satisfy those of a speculative turn of mind living securely in the towns but they are hardly enough to bring comfort to the hearts and souls of those living lives of grinding toil back in the bush. Superficial gratification is not enough. Something deeper is required and sought after. For many, the search has ended in a Methodist camp meeting.

Although smaller than some, the recent meeting near St Thomas is typical of those that have taken place in the backwoods of Upper Canada during the past three or four decades. As is the custom, it was held in the fall after the crops were in and the geese were flying south. High overhead their lonely honking only emphasized the growing silence of the forest – winter was approaching. Here and there along the rough, rutted roads could be heard the creaking axles, bumping wheels, the clip-clop of horses, and peals of laughter as groups of people trundled along towards the open space set aside for the meeting. As the distance shortened, anticipation mounted until at last the place set aside for the horses and wagons was reached. The devout and the curious then set off on foot to cover the last mile to the meeting site. There was nothing of the solemnness of parishioners walking to church but rather the mirth and fun of a rare trip to a country fair. When they finally emerged at the clearing, they found logs laid out in parallel rows for seating five or six hundred people. Surrounding this central square were tents where they would live together for the next four or five days. As darkness fell, soft candles began to flicker in the tents but in the square, brightness returned with the lighting of several huge fires – including one six-feet high near the speakers' platform. The scene was completely enchanting as the flaming reds, oranges, and yellows of the autumn leaves overhead attempted to outdo in brilliance the very fires themselves. As the sparks rose towards heaven, singing commenced and the preacher, Brother Fraiser, grew hoarse in his exhortations to the assembled multitudes to come forth and be relieved of their sins.

Some meetings last a week or ten days and are attended by as many as 3000 people. It is considered nothing to travel more than a hundred miles to take part. After a year of routine and drudgery, the excitement of the camp meeting is eagerly looked forward to, even by the women who must prepare food in advance for a week or more, and especially by the young people who, although they may not have been allowed to attend a dance or concert, are permitted to mix freely with other youth without censure. Perhaps the boy or girl of their dreams will be there!

According to the author of a letter in the Chatham *Weekly Journal*, prejudice against camp meetings was running high in 1841, and it was this prejudice which had decided him to indulge his "natural curiosity" by a visit to "test the truth of the assertion of scandalizing the world." He was pleasantly surprised by what he saw and heard – there were nine preachers present and "the whole devotions were conducted in a systematic manner ... several very excellent sermons were preached to a congregation of about 1500 souls."

The camp meeting was not the only popular diversion under attack in 1841. There is another, praised by some for the good results it produces and condemned by others for the evil that attends it. It too is the product of newly settled areas and also reflects the levelling system of America. Like the camp meeting, people are drawn to it with all the enthusiasm of peasants running to a race course or fair. It is noted for its bustle and activity – and that is why it is generally known as a *bee*.

Bees are gatherings for carrying out specific tasks. There are logging bees, husking bees, barn-raising bees, and a number of other bees – depending on what needs to be done. Bees evolved in the new settlements of America where labour was scarce and, hence, expensive. Rather than compete for the few workers who were available, settlers got together to help one another. When a bee is "called," forty or fifty men will gather in time for breakfast at the home of the host. The work is then portioned out – the most important job going to the "grog-boss," who is in charge of the whiskey. His is no sinecure. Throughout the day he will be constantly in demand as he wanders the work site with a pail of water and a dipper in one hand and a bottle of whiskey in the other. There are breaks for tea, and at noon and again in the evening the pine-board tables are loaded with lamb, mutton, suckling pig, vegetables, preserves, pies, puddings, beer, whiskey, and tea. After supper there is always a frolic, often in the form of contests – running, jumping, wrestling, putting the shot, and throwing the hammer – that enable the men to show off their physical prowess. Settlers who are known to be poor can usually get away with providing only the whiskey and the frolic.

If all goes well, the men will leave at dusk, happy with a good day's work and pleasure behind them, and the host satisfied with the results of their voluntary labour. If all does not go well – and this is often the case – both host and workers will ponder whether or not to take part in future bees. Largely because of the staggering amount of alcohol consumed, accidents are numerous, some resulting in death. Quarrels are common, some ending in murder or manslaughter. The quality of work is generally poor and productivity is low. The host has little control over who shows up and so is liable to be plagued with riff-raff who spend their days going from bee to bee, indulging in all the pleasures but doing no work. Some now argue that it is more economical to hire a few real labourers at high wages than to provide food and drink for a small army of workers, most of whom just stand around and get into one another's way. Once involved, however, it is difficult to avoid taking part in bees because the host is obligated to help all who had helped him should they also call a bee. The result, in the eyes of some, is a continual round of drunkenness and dissipation. For heavy tasks such as rais-

BEES

Like the camp meeting, the bee was part of the levelling process of America. The new-found independence of the settler was not compromised – there were no wages and no bosses – and if he were from the lower ranks of society (and most were) he was allowed to forget his origin. It made no difference whether his father had been a labourer out for hire or an independent settler, a poor artisan or an educated gentleman, a soldier or an officer: in the bee they all came together in shirtless sweat for the public good and a common carouse. Settlers with social pretensions quickly recognized that one's station in society meant little in the backwoods, that other men worked *with* one and not *for* one, and that the customary rules of society no longer applied. The absence of normal conventions could, on some occasions, greatly ease social relationships, but on others it could lead to disputes, misunderstandings, and even to violence.

ing barns, bees are indispensible, but it is wise to attempt to restrict the number of workers to about thirty-five and to serve no drink until after the work is done.

The levelling influence of bees, camp meetings, and the like is felt most keenly in newly settled areas in the bush. Half-pay officers and gently nurtured ladies like Susan Mein Sibbald have found it almost impossible to maintain class distinctions in such an uncouth environment. Mrs Sibbald is presently living at Eildon Hall, her estate near Jackson's Point on Lake Simcoe, a long way from the fashionable school in Bath where she was educated, from London, where she spent the winters after her debut, and from Scotland where she summered at her father's estate in the borders. At Eildon Hall she receives members of the Toronto aristocracy. Undoubtedly a favourite topic of conversation is the decline of the old values.*

"The season" in Canada is conveniently bracketed by St Andrew's Day, which marks the closing of the St Lawrence (and the slowing down of commercial life in the towns and cities), and by St George's Day, which usually coincides with the reopening of the river. Traditionally, St Andrew's Day on 30 November is marked with a ball. The custom goes all the way back to the Conquest. In 1764, the year Canada was actually transferred to the British, "every person and Family in the city [of Quebec] and neighbourhood, of suitable rank, as well as his Majesty's new subjects as old, was invited." Between St Andrew's Day and St George's Day on 23 April a number of winter assemblies were customarily held, but during the difficulties of the past few years they had been allowed to die out. Late in 1841, however, the assemblies were being revived and it is hoped that by bringing all parties together, they will "soften the bitterness of political strife."

During the first of these new assemblies it was pleasant indeed to see the military, professions, merchants, and others freely mingling under the brilliant light of numerous candles "burning without fear of cost." It was a grand opportunity for ladies to display their finery as they promenaded or danced the night away. For those who do not dance – and about half of those present do not – there were cards, conversation, and refreshments. Perhaps there will be more dancers at the four other assemblies planned before spring now that Miss Steward has established her academy – over Mr Drysdale's shop next to the market – for the purpose of "teaching danc-

---

* Like Susanna Moody and her husband (a half-pay officer), Mrs Sibbald would eventually move into town where at least the possibility remained for the preservation of the social fabric.

ing in all its fashionable variety, consisting in Quadrilles, minuets, Gavottes &c. &c."

Now that Kingston has replaced Quebec and Toronto as the Canadian metropolis, dancing there is also becoming *de rigueur*. Lessons in the "usual routine of Ball-room" as well as the "Victoria, Gallonade, Caledonian, and Lancers' Quadrilles, Mazourkas, and Circassian Circles" are being offered by J. Crerar in the new stone building on Rear Street, known as the Athenaeum. Like Quebec, Kingston is fortunate in having a garrison. It not only provides bands for dancing but also young officers from respectable families for the young ladies of the town with social ambitions. In 1841 Quebec women were probably the more fortunate. Stationed in their midst are battalions of two of the oldest and most distinguished British regiments – the Grenadier and Coldstream guards. (Among the officers who are enduring the bedbugs of rented quarters in the city is Robert Peel Dawson, close relative of Sir Robert Peel, the British prime minister.) Few civilians can contend with the lavish hospitality the guards are able to offer their friends and the fashionables of Quebec. Who could compete with the party given in February by the Coldstream Guards in their St Louis Street barracks where the mess-hall was converted into a ballroom and other areas prepared for cards, refreshments, and as a supper room? And who could hope to equal the Grenadier Guards with their entertainment a week later at the Citadel barracks? Besides dancing and the choicest refreshments, they offered a performance by Alexandre Vattemare, the famous French ventriloquist and philanthropist. And who could offer such extravagant use of light? There were variegated lamps, Chinese lanterns, waxed candles in chandeliers, candelabra composed of muskets standing on pedestals, and transparencies displaying the names of glorious scenes of service of the Grenadiers. Certainly not the common soldier, who was probably getting drunk in some dark tavern while all of this was going on. His place is with members of the labouring class and, like them, his only recreation is that of the dram-shops and the canteen. The balls, concerts, receptions, and picnic parties that flow during "the season" are not for him.

In summer, the common soldiers *are* permitted to attend the races at Quebec – they can be seen keeping the track clear while the officers and gentry look on from the stands. Unlike the race course at Montreal, the Quebec track is not protected by a high barrier. This allows fashionable ladies, who do not wish to be crushed in the stands, to view the races from their carriages. It is a wonderful opportunity to see and to be seen, but against this advantage must be weighed the damage that might be caused to the complexion by the sun and the dust.

RACING

Everyone loved a good race, from the habitant out-
distancing his neighbour on the way home from church
to the ladies and gentlemen of the Quebec Driving
Club who could be seen wrapped in furs as they bumped
around Place d'Armes in their little carioles – bells tinkling
and runners squeaking on the snow. Even the smallest
boy with a dog sled had to see just how fast he could go.
When the St Lawrence froze over completely – it happened
about one year in ten – there was great excitement as
people with their skates, horses, sleds, and sleighs went
down to the river to celebrate the event. At Montreal,
Kingston, and Toronto, the harbours froze every
year and were the scenes of much amusement.

Racing is among the diversions sometimes criticized because of "the low and degrading passions" it can call up. The same cannot be said of curling. According to James Bicket, secretary of the Toronto Curling Club, "no betting ever takes place [and] ... intoxication on the ice is also unknown among good players." Perhaps the Presbyterian church deserves some of the credit for the seriousness and the sobriety of this sport. In Scotland it is generally the local minister who is among the most enthusiastic supporters of curling. In Newmarket (and probably elsewhere in Canada as well) it is no surprise to find the minister – "an exact and skillful player" – actively promoting the game. Curling is by no means restricted to Scots in Canada, al-

---

SUBLIME EXPERIMENT AT NIAGARA FALLS

Perhaps the crudest bit of entertainment arose from the "sublime experiment" that took place at Niagara Falls in September 1841. A condemned ship, the *Detroit*, captured by the Americans during the War of 1812 and recently rechristened the *Veto* (as a warning to President Tyler, elected in 1841, who was then at loggerheads with the House), was furnished with a crew of live animals for a voyage over the falls. Thousands assembled on both sides to watch the spectacle. Unhappily for the promoters, the ship was too close to the American shore and, after upsetting, became stuck fast on the rocks above the falls – a perfect example of the juxtaposition of the sublime and the ridiculous so often noted at Niagara Falls.

---

though it is more common in areas with large Scottish populations. For some Canadians the sweeping of a stone thrown down the ice on a cold winter's day might be a cause for laughter. Fortunately, the muted sense of humour of the Scot has allowed the game to become firmly established on this side of the Atlantic.

Canada's more southerly location and colder climate make it a much better country for curling than Scotland. Not only are the winters colder but the days are longer and sunnier. The Scottish lochs and ponds freeze only for brief periods, compelling enthusiasts to curl from dawn to dusk. In Canada the ice can be depended upon for weeks at a time. This means that curlers can play an hour here and an hour there whenever time will allow. Even in Toronto, where the climate is comparatively mild, the season often lasts for three months. Dependable ice has made possible distant competitions or bonspiels. For example, early in 1841 the Quebec curling club travelled the 180 miles to Montreal "with their curling stones on their back, to contend for three days, in friendly strife, for the master." Last year half the players of each club travelled to the opposite city, where joint matches were held on the same day. A few years before that the bonspiel had been held at Trois-Rivières, the midway point. As curlers begin to journey further afield in competition, the need for a common set of written rules is becoming more apparent.

In Scotland the Grand Caledonia Club of Edinburgh recently attempted to regulate the proportions of stones used in curling, but in the Canadas a wide variety of shapes, weights, and materials are still in use. Some are made to slide on either of the flattened surfaces – one slightly concave for hard ice and the other convex for ice that is soft and dull. A hard stone, free of sand, such as granite, is best. This can be obtained in the Toronto area, although stones imported from Scotland are played along side those produced locally. At Montreal and Quebec, where colliding stones are liable to break in the intense cold, iron castings in the shape of curling stones are used. At Guelph suitable rock for stones is unavailable and so the game is played with blocks of hard wood. At Fergus similar blocks are loaded with lead.

Sweeping is an important part of curling. Not only does it keep the players from freezing to death but it is said to influence the movement of the stones. In Scotland the brooms are usually made locally from "broom" but sometimes birch twigs or heather are substituted. In Canada corn [straw] brooms are found to be acceptable – provided they have been well used at home first so that no knotty parts might break off and slow the stone – thus giving the women of the household the satisfaction of making an important contribution to the game. At Scarborough, near Toronto, a group of enthusiastic curlers from Lanarkshire have begun to cultivate genuine Scotch broom. It is thriving and in the future promises to supersede all other materials used for brooms.

Curling is played in the open air during a time of year when few other outdoor pleasures can be enjoyed. Scottish immigrants accustomed to the fresh air within the buildings of their homeland are happy to escape from the enfeebling effects of close and overheated Canadian houses. Sleigh rides, snowshoeing, tobogganing, skating, and winter picnics are other antidotes to what the Canadians refer to as cabin fever. For those who prefer indoors diversions there are the regular theatrical productions of the garrisons, soirées, card games, and chess.

During the present winter, several well-dressed gentlemen are regularly seen carrying chess boards as they hurry along the unlit streets of Quebec. They are on their way to the newly formed Quebec Chess Club that meets regularly at Payne's Hotel. When the sky

---

TOBOGGANING

In winter, fashionable Quebeckers clad in furs could be seen gliding over the ice of the St Lawrence in their light carioles on their way to Montmorency to visit the falls and to ascend the ice cone – a "sugar loaf" that was created by the freezing spray and the accumulating layers of snow. Many an exhilarating hour was spent in sliding down its steep slopes.

---

is clear and the light from the stars or moon is reflected from the gleaming snow, the men are able to pick their way along the narrow streets and lanes with little difficulty. (There is something comforting about the night air filled with the smoke of hundreds of wood fires.) Like other diversions of a more refined nature, chess has had difficulty in competing with the more sensual pleasures of the winter season. This has also been the experience of the Literary and Historical Society of Quebec, the city's chief forum for the speculative and philosophical mind.

Attendance at the meetings of the Literary and Historical Society in 1841 has been most disappointing and in the society's annual report it was reluctantly concluded that many members of the official and military class were more concerned with the gratification of the senses than with the elevation of the mind and spirit. Many of its members have not paid their contributions and the society is deeply in debt to its treasurer. Unhappily, this is not a novel situation for a society that has found over the years that seldom does

Coasting Down the Cone, Montmorency Falls, by Mrs M.M. Chaplin. Watercolour, NAC

THE LITERARY AND HISTORICAL
SOCIETY OF QUEBEC

The Literary and Historical Society of Quebec was founded in 1824 under the auspices of the governor, Lord Dalhousie. Its members were chiefly gentlemen of high official rank in the province. Three years later a similar institution, the Society for the Encouragement of Arts and Sciences in Canada, was formed by a number of gentlemen who were anxious to "produce a literary and scientific stimulus among persons professionally qualified to extend the influence of works of genius and taste." In 1829 both organizations were combined as the Society for Promoting Literature, Science, Arts and Historical Research in Canada. This unwieldy title soon gave way to the restoration of the old name, the Literary and Historical Society of Quebec. This brief history helps to explain why the scope of the society's interests were much broader than its name implied. This breadth might be best illustrated by listing the papers presented in 1841: Notes on the Labrador Coast; On the Natural History of the American Bear; On the Causes of Diseases among Emigrants Coming to this Country; On the Importance of a General System of Education in Canada; Some Observations on the Discriminating Power of the Human Ear; On an Epidemic Disease in this Country, Eighty Years Ago; Notices on the Natural History of the Minobranchus Lateralis; Notes on the History of Alchymy; and An Analysis of the Water of the Georgian Spring on the Ottawa.

In the bylaws of the society, its objects were divided into four classes:

I. Literature and history, to comprehend: moral philosophy, philology, polite and fine arts, literature generally, civil history, antiquities, geography, statistics, political economy.

II. Natural history: zoology, geology, mineralogy, meteorology, botany, and dendrology.

III. Science: astronomy, mathematics, chemistry, natural and experimental philosophy.

IV. Arts: agriculture, commerce, trade, manufacturers, mechanics, domestic and useful arts.

For each class, chairmen were appointed who had over the years with varying degrees of success endeavoured to stimulate interest in their assigned fields by means of lectures, essay prizes, and the society's museum. Generally their efforts had met with only modest success. Part of the reason may have been because members of the official class from which the society still drew most of its members were frequently transferred from Quebec to other parts of the empire, but more likely because they were unable to "spare an hour from the usual entertainments of the season" for intellectual improvement.

Youth especially might gain from the exertions of the society – particularly in the field of natural history which was, in the words of a former chairman of that section, "so admirably calculated to occupy their leisure hours agreeably and usefully, to embellish and enlarge, as well as to invigorate their understanding: and above all to purify their taste, and to awaken in them a relish for some of the highest enjoyments of which we are susceptible." Not only would such studies please the inquiring mind but they would also be of great practical benefit to the people as a whole as newly discovered knowledge led to the improvement of agriculture, or as new purposes were found for the plants and minerals in which Canada abounded.

One of the most beneficial results of the exertions of the Literary and Historical Society of Quebec and that of its sister society in Montreal was the founding of the Geological Survey of the Province of Canada in 1841. (After Confederation it became the Geological Survey of Canada and continued its important work down to the present day.)

its finances or its intellectual attainments measure up to its ambitions. For example, in 1836 it was reported that "no part of the Society's attempts" was so unsuccessful "as the endeavour to call forth the intellectual energies of the country by the offer of prizes." From first to last, this attempt had been a failure.

NEPAL RICE

On at least one occasion the Literary and Historical Society of Quebec experimented with the introduction of exotic plants. This was in 1839 when it received from Sir John Colborne a parcel of mountain rice "in order that they might institute experiments as to its fitness for cultivation in Canada, and endeavor to ascertain whether any benefit was likely to be derived from its introduction into general culture in these provinces." The parcel was accompanied with a copy of a letter from Lord Glenelg to His Excellency which stated that the grain had been raised in "Napaul [sic] at the foot of the Himmaleh [sic] mountains," in a climate considered to resemble very closely that of the Canadas. He also referred to information respecting the mode of cultivating it that was to be found in papers in the *Transactions of the Society of Arts*. Small quantities of the rice were distributed to several gentlemen interested in agriculture. It was sown with and without previous preparation, in greenhouses and in the open air, in flooded soils and in ordinary ones, but in no instance did it show the least sign of germinating. The grain seemed to have been spoiled in some way.

"The all engrossing subject of politics seems to have carried mens' minds from the peaceful pursuits of science and literature" during recent years and interest in the society has reached a low ebb. However, it is hoped that with tranquility having been restored to the province there will be a return to pursuits which, "while they tend to enlarge the minds of those engaged in them, give offence to none and are more or less for the benefit of all." Membership in the society is open to all, but in practice most of its members are from the

DAGUERREOTYPE

Nature and nature's God were also put to good use by the itinerant Daguerreotype artists who began touring Canada in 1840, only a year after the photographic process was first introduced in France. Unlike the then popular miniature portraits from the hand of man, Daguerreotypes were truly "the pencilings of nature." One could not help but be in awe as nature's sun etched the plate. Perhaps this accounted in part for the gravity of expression of early Daguerreotypes. The required length of exposure may also have had something to do with it. Two long minutes were required for a Montreal sitting in June 1841. Since it was necessary to make the pictures out-of-doors, Daguerreotyping was a source of entertainment to passers-by who must have been tempted to bring smiles to the sitter's face. (It would be many decades before a smile was acceptable in a photograph.) The Daguerreotypes made in 1841 were considered quite satisfactory – much better than those obtained during the previous autumn when the sun was weaker and the image less pronounced. No pictures could be made on rainy or overcast days.

Daguerreotype artists were sometimes called professors, especially if they were prepared to teach the art and sell the required apparatus to pupils. The apparatus, together with a short period of training, provided the modern man or woman (of no particular talent) with a medium for acquiring a measure of independence and respectability. For a spirited woman, the Daguerreotype offered possibilities that would remain unequalled until the coming of the typewriter a few decades later.

Photography soon placed the gifted miniaturist in the same position as the unemployed hand-loom worker. Who would now set aside a few hours for an expensive miniature when a Daguerreotype could be obtained at one-fifth the cost in only a few minutes stolen from a busy day?

upper ranks of society, civil and military. In 1841 only a few French names appear in the list of members – perhaps a reflection of the "all engrossing subject of politics."

TALKING MACHINE

One 10 April 1841 the *Quebec Mercury* reported a device even more wonderful than the Daguerreotype – a talking machine was said to have been invented by a Manchester man.
Since it could report speakers verbatim, wine-warmed orators would no longr be able to throw the reporter overboard when they got into scrapes.

Since its foundation, the Literary and Historical Society has occupied rooms in the Union Building on Place d'Armes at Fort Street. The building was owned by the chief justice and leased to the government for the offices of the principal departments of Lower Canada. With the move to Kingston, the lease is being terminated and the society is casting about for new quarters.

The society's museum in the Union Building remained open during 1841 for the reception of "persons of taste and science." Although gratified by an inspection of its varied contents, visitors were dismayed by the telltale signs of neglect and the general disorder of the collection. It is difficult to make sense of the catch-all jumble of geological specimens, shells, medals, prints, maps, "curious objects," books, and manuscripts. A list of donations made to the museum during 1841 allows a savouring of the collection as a whole. These included a 1771 £3 bank note from the Colony of New York, thirty-six preserved botanical specimens, a 1691 Hanovarian coin, two lampreys from the St Lawrence preserved in spirits, a specimen of raised printing for the use of the blind, as well as a great variety of books.

The society had intended to publish its transactions annually. Although this objective has not always been met, several creditable volumes have appeared. In addition, one of its members, the Rev. Mr Holmes of the Quebec Seminary, has produced what is believed to be the first complete work of geography composed and published in North America. No pains were spared in making his *Géogra-*

MUSEUM OF THE LITERARY
AND HISTORICAL SOCIETY OF QUEBEC

"There were the usual objects of a museum here – common things putting on the wonderful by dint of hard name and particular date, labels with the name of the donor more conspicuous than that of the gift, showing a love of ostentation rather than of science. Monstrosities made more monstrous and inexplicable by the distorting powers of the glass bottles, others rendered indiscernible and unnatural by the thickness of the spirits etc. However, the museum, considering its age, is a promising youth."

The Canadian Journal of Alfred Domett, ed. E.A. Horsman and Lillian Rae Benson, p. 9

JOSEPH LÉGARÉ

One of the most active members of the Literary and Historical Society of Quebec was Joseph Légaré, the painter, who became chairman of the arts class in 1832. For several years he allowed his large personal collection of European canvases to hang on public view in the rooms of the society. As an artist, Légaré painted a great variety of works, including several events from contemporary life such as the cholera epidemic at Quebec (see p. 99) and the 1841 rock fall at Cape Diamond (see p. 27). Considered the first landscape artist of French-Canadian origin, he drew heavily on the English topographical painters and their liking for picturesque views. That is probably why his work was popular among officer of the British garrison, who formed part of his clientele. Nevertheless, Légaré was an admirer of Louis-Joseph Papineau and in 1837 he became caught up in the "all engrossing" activities of the Quebec Patriotes. He was arrested on 13 November and jailed for five days before being set free on bail. As an ardent nationalist, he opposed the union of 1841.

phie Moderne as complete and as correct as possible. The minute details that are given respecting the present state of population, trade, government, and recent discoveries are ample proof of the diligence and research that were employed in its compilation.

For tradesmen and artisans who might not feel at ease in the Literary and Historical Society, there is a mechanics's institute. It has its own rooms and a library but it is not in a flourishing state. Members are few, means are limited, and the establishment is apparently just as neglected as that of the older and wealthier society. Fortunately, readers in Quebec are not totally dependent upon the libraries in the society and the institute. There are several other libraries in the city, including the Quebec Library, which contains "a great variety of standard and interesting works in both English and French" and an excellent library for the use of the garrison. Where books are available, the more ambitious can teach themselves. That is how thirty-four-year-old Joseph Casavant, "a blacksmith with music in his soul," has learned to build organs. From a parish priest he borrowed works on his craft, including Dom François Bédor de Celles's enormous treatise *L'art du facteur d'orgues*. During the past year Casavant has been in St Hyacinthe building an organ for the parish church of St Martin on Ile Jésus.

Much of what has been said of Quebec could also be said of its larger rival, Montreal. It, too, has its winter assemblies, its clubs, and its libraries. The Natural History Society of Montreal is a sister institution of the Literary and Historical Society of Quebec. Both societies have kindred aims and draw their memberships from similar ranks of society.

Intellectual life in the newer and smaller cities of Upper Canada is less flourishing. In Toronto there is a literary club and a mechanics' institute but, as yet, neither has created much interest. According to Anna Jameson, "absolutely the only place of assembly or amusement, except the taverns and low drinking-houses," is the commercial newsroom. Yet, even in Toronto there is to be found evidence of the improving spirit at work: there are now two good bookstores; both have been established recently and one even provides a circulating library of two or three hundred volumes. Perhaps this may be taken as a sign that diversions of a more refined and innocent nature are becoming increasingly available in the Canadas.

Chapter VI

Immigrants, Optimism, and Future Prospects

The year 1841 ended in a buoyant spirit of confidence. Agriculture was reviving, exports were up, and 6000 more immigrants had arrived than in the previous year. During the "open season" between early May and September, nearly 30,000 newcomers had poured in from Great Britain and Ireland. Pessimism about their prospects in the old country may have led them to emigrate, but their arrival in Canada inspired optimism among the old residents of Canada, especially among those of British background. They saw in the immigrants a source of capital and labour which, when applied to the vast "wastelands" of Canada, would produce wealth for everyone, newcomer and native alike. Speculators with large holdings of land were especially heartened. Without labour, they said, the land had no value – as had been the case during the past few years when the uncertainties caused by the rebellions and their aftermath had reduced the flow of immigrants. This, in turn, had contributed to the serious downturn in the economy. That the flow was in full spate once more signaled not only a return to greater prosperity but an end to the troubled times. Even more encouraging was the fact that more of the migrants were remaining in Canada rather than continuing on to the United States.

As would be expected, French-Canadian politicians were much less enthusiastic about the introduction of so many British settlers. Not only was their own position being threatened politically but a real danger existed that in the future there would be insufficient land to support the burgeoning French-Canadian population. They were becoming hemmed in on both the east and the west. American settlers from the south were encroaching in the Eastern Townships and, in the west, they were being outflanked by the rapid growth of the English colony of Upper Canada. Statements by men like John Beverley Robinson, a descendant of a Loyalist family and chief justice of Upper Canada, did little to assuage their fears. He said that French-Canadian politicians might believe they had a right to have the province to themselves but "some thousands of industrious and loyal emigrants from Ireland, and the Highlands of Scotland, would check such absurd ideas of nationality as effectually as a military force."

In Lower Canada the system of landholding and the density of settlement in the seigniorial lands along the St Lawrence had largely shielded the French-Canadian community from the newcomers, but even here some British settlers had bought land – particularly near Quebec and Montreal where they would be well situated for the local markets and could have access in the cities to the most sophisticated English society in the Canadas. Although these lands were by now considerably exhausted through many years of cultivation, they could be brought back through an infusion of capital and modern British farming techniques. A few settlers chose the Eastern Townships, which also had the advantage of being relatively close to the markets of Montreal and Quebec, but most went on to Upper Canada or the United States, notwithstanding the considerable effort being made by the authorities to induce immigrants to settle in Lower Canada.

Whether Upper Canada or the United States was the better place to settle was a matter of considerable discussion. Upper Canada, most people seemed to agree, was the better poor man's country, while the United States was more suited to the man of some little capital. In the United States he could buy land cheaply, trade with any part of the world, and look forward to his children's rising to the highest offices in the country if they had the ability. In the older parts of the United States, railways, canals, and reasonably good roads made it possible for the farmer to take his surplus to local markets. In Upper Canada, with a much smaller and more scattered population, such markets were few and far between – greatly reducing the settler's opportunities for enriching himself and his family. However, it was easier for the poor man to acquire land in Upper Canada than in the United States. If he worked hard, assisted by a family of sons, he might erect a rough cabin and gradually clear an amount of land sufficient for his family's subsistence. In time he could rise to affluence, although only to the affluence of a labourer. For the man of capital, Upper Canada was less attractive because it did not pay to invest in improving unsettled land; once improved, the land was worth less than the cost of improvement. Yet, if in spite of this, he chose to settle in Upper

Canada, he could live quite comfortably but he would not rise
in life.

In some areas, including the Eastern Townships where the Yankee axeman was active, it was possible to purchase land with ten,
twenty, thirty, or more acres already cleared for less money than
wild land. "Cleared land" might conjure up visions of "smiling
fields" back in Britain but in reality it usually meant a patch here
and a patch there marred by huge fire-blackened stumps, four
feet high. Provided the land had been recently cleared, the settler
could at least see what he was buying. Otherwise, the space among
the stumps would be obscured by a luxuriant growth of underbrush whose height indicated how long the area had been cleared.
Governor Sir Francis Bond Head was always deeply affected in
"passing these little monuments of the failure of human expectations – the blight of human hopes!" Frequently the stumps were so
close together that it was impossible to use a plough, forcing the
settler to revert to primitive sowing and hand-raking. Wooded land
meant the backbreaking task of clearing before discovering whether
the soil was good or bad. It was said that bad land was harder to
clear than good land and that this fulfilled the old Yankee proverb,
"it is like a bad horse, hard to be caught, and when caught, good
for nothing."

By 1841 land was available in Canada only through sale. Earlier
it had been granted gratuitously, but when it was taken up by
poor people it was found that they neither had the means of living
while waiting for their crops to mature nor much idea of how to
farm in the Canadas. Thus, they were forced to work for wages
until they accumulated a few savings while at the same time trying
to learn something about farming in Canada. Now land was sold
on the open market at a moderate price. An argument against free
land was that it lessened the supply of labour and thus raised its
price. High wages, in turn, discouraged capital. Thus, free land discouraged capital investment. In 1841 the poor immigrant was expected to work for wages (as he had done before) *and then* buy
his land. He would thus appreciate his holding more and only the
"industrious and sober" would become landowners. Those who
were lazy and unsteady would fail to accumulate the savings necessary to purchase land. This was all to the good since they would unlikely make good settlers anyway. It was said that wages were
higher in Canada than in Britain and the industrious immigrant
could expect to earn enough in a few seasons to become a free-
holder. If the newcomer were to gain his wages by working for an
experienced farmer, he would, at the same time, be able to learn

the art of farming in Canada. Even if, like Joseph Abbott of St Andrew's, Lower Canada, he had farmed back in Great Britain, he still had much to learn. Abbott, like most English farmers newly arrived in Canada, had felt that he had a great deal to teach but little to learn from the locals. He soon discovered, however, that those around him had little confidence in him as a teacher. "How should they," he later admitted, "when [I] did not even know how to cut a tree down, or to hoe a hill of Indian corn, the very first things a farmer's boy, in this country, learns."

Those who had been cotters or small tenants on large estates in the old country were generally reluctant to take up agricultural employment working for others in Canada, especially since the wages offered were often insufficient to support a family in comfort. Without hired hands, farmers lacking active children found it difficult to make progress. At the same time, there were many landless men wandering from place to place looking for work. They preferred labouring on public works such as fortifications and canals to farming because the pay was better. However, because of the severe Canadian climate, most of this work (like farming) was seasonal and, during the long, dreary, unemployed winter, they suffered from cold, hunger, and pauperism. They lived from year to year, congregating around the cities without improving their condition. Eventually, many of them left the country altogether. Future opportunities for buying land were not enough to hold them.

The fact that one could always move on made it impossible to transplant British social arrangements to Canada. Any attempt to force on the Canadian community the master-servant, capitalist-labourer relationships of the old country was in vain. The attempt might succeed in a new country such as New Zealand, where the poor man could not escape, but it would never succeed in the Canadas. It was far too easy to move on to the United States. And many immigrants did just that.

To encourage more immigrants to remain in the Canadas, emigrant agents were appointed in the larger cities and towns. (That the newcomers were usually considered "emigrants" rather than immigrants in the Canadas of 1841 indicated that the English-Canadian mind was still fixed in the British Isles.) Their task was to enable the newcomer to settle in Canada as smoothly as possible. They set up emigrant sheds and hospitals, they helped with matters respecting the acquisition of land, and they brought the newcomers together with persons requesting farm servants, labourers, craftsmen, and other workers. Emigration associations were also formed in various parts of the country to carry out similar duties. Like the agents, their concern was to keep as many migrants in their own region as possible; no matter how poor the migrant might be on arrival, immigration was equated with prosperity. Holding on to the immigrant was not easy in Lower Canada, which was viewed by most immigrants merely as being along the route to Upper Canada. The problem was made worse by rumours then circulating in Britain that painted a rosy picture of Upper Canada as a land of high wages. While it was true in 1841 that there was a demand for tradesmen and farm servants in Upper Canada, there was an oversupply of unskilled labourers. Yet, attempts to persuade the unskilled among the immigrants to stay and work on the roads in Montreal and Quebec met with little success, so effective were the rumours about Upper Canada. As a result, many unskilled workers were arriving in Upper Canada penniless (having expended their meager savings in moving up country), without any prospects for work. To help alleviate the hardship facing the unemployed in Upper Canada, public works were initiated such as the one begun at Kingston in June 1841 for raising and breaking stone near the town. Those with skills stood a better chance of escaping from poverty. They might even follow in the footsteps of John Redpath and Thomas McKay, two young stonemasons who had emigrated from Scotland a quarter of a century earlier. By 1841 both were successful merchants, having established their fortunes by contracting for work on the locks, first on the Lachine and then on the Rideau canals. Both would go on to create a number of enterprises that would enrich themselves and the Canadas, including Redpath's sugar refinery at Montreal, the first in the country. Meanwhile, thousands of other migrants were taking up land in the bush and laboriously adding to its value as they transformed it into farms. Their efforts, along with the restoration of political stability, were, indeed, reasons for optimism about the future of the Canadas.

The new year, 1842, dawned in a flurry of illuminations in Toronto, Bytown, and other Canadian centres in honour of the birth of the Prince of Wales. (After a certain amount of dissention, Quebec somewhat belatedly celebrated the event with a ball.) Meanwhile, His Excellency Sir Charles Bagot, the new governor general, had arrived in New York on the *HMS Illustrious* on 30 December 1841. He was to begin his winter journey to the Canadas on 3 January 1842. His arrival in the United States underlined the fact that, in winter, Canada experienced all the difficulties of a land-locked country. This inconvenience was pointed out in a very generous article in praise of the united Canadas in *The Novascotian* in August 1841. Unlike the lower provinces, the Canadas lacked two important elements for prosperity – open harbours and a homogenous population.

The Novascotian was overawed by the sheer magnitude of the Canadas: "From Anticosti to Quebec is about 600 miles, and then, when you have got there, you are but upon the threshold of the Province. For two days and nights you steam along, after entering the estuary of the St Lawrence, at the *Unicorn*'s highest speed, with Canada on both sides of you; and, when you are beneath the shadow of Cape Diamond, you begin to think you have got a reasonable distance inland." Yet Kingston, the capital, was a thousand miles from the sea and one could travel westward another thousand miles and still be in Canada. *The Novascotian* suggested that the grandeur of the natural features of the Canadas might be able to elevate the spirit of the people above "the scene of perpetual discord and degradation" and inspire them with the union, virtue, and true patriotism. As they would say in the United States, Canada was "considerable of a place." Whether its people were worthy of their inheritance, only the future would tell.

Afterword

Ian Alexander Bell Robertson returned to Scotland, where he lived in active retirement until he died at the age of eighty in 1851. He retained an interest in Canada and frequently entertained Canadian visitors in his Edinburgh home, including a number of students training to become doctors or ministers. He learned from them that the union had not been a complete success and, now, it was Upper Canada rather than Lower Canada that felt the more aggrieved by the arrangement. From the distant perspective of Edinburgh, Canadian squabbles seemed very petty and Robertson never could understand why so few people living in such a vast country could not get along with one another.

Politics bored Robertson and he was far more interested in hearing his visitors tell about the rapid growth of Montreal and Toronto and how quickly the peninsula of southern Upper Canada was being settled. When he had sailed for Scotland in 1842, the population of Upper Canada was 450,000 – triple what it had been in 1825. At the time of his death in 1851, it had doubled again. Toronto was by then 30,000 – more twice the size of Hamilton and almost three times the size of Kingston. As had happened earlier in Edinburgh, civic amenity was being sacrificed in the name of progress. He had seen the North Loch between the Old and New Towns drained, planted in a garden, and then despoiled by a polluting railway. Now there was talk of running a railway along Toronto's beautiful lake front.

Quebec's optimistic prediction that it would regain its position of primacy was not realized. Montreal continued to outpace it in growth and by 1851 was a third larger. Montreal's more central location, the improvement of the canals, and the building of railways in the 1840s all contributed to its growth.

Robertson fondly remembered his stay in the Canadas. If Quebec had reminded him of Edinburgh, then Edinburgh reminded him of Quebec. A visit to the Lawn Market evoked memories of Upper Town Market, the air filled with wood smoke and the babble of broken English and bad French. A trip down the Forth to Portobello or Musselburgh conjured up visions of the road to Montmorency, the little whitewashed houses with the turned-up eaves and the windows filled with flowers. A whiff of pine brought back scenes of rivers and lakes with huge trees coming right down to the water's edge. That remained his dominant memory of the Canadas even though, in many places, it was no longer so.

Bibliography

Abbott, Joseph. *The Emigrant to North America*. Edinburgh and London 1844

Abdy, Edward Strutt. *Journal of a Residence and Tour in the United States of North America, 1833, to October, 1834*, 3 vols. London 1835

Abrahamson, Une. *Domestic Life in Nineteenth Century Canada*. Sault Ste Marie 1975

Abrégéde la Géographie du Canada à l'usage des écoles de cette Province. Montréal: Imprimé par Ludger Duvernay 1831

Agreement between the Hon. S. Cunard and H.M.'s Government for conveying mails by steam, reports on the subject of a daily mail communication between Halifax and St. John, etc. *Journals of the New Brunswick House of Assembly, 1841*, appendix, clv-clxix

The Albion. New York 1841

Alexander, Sir James Edward. *Transatlantic Sketches, Comprising Visits to the Most Interesting Scenes in North and South America, and the West Indies. With Notes on Negro Slavery and Canadian Emigration*, 2 vols. London 1833

Allardice, Robert Barclay. *Agricultural Tour of the United States and Upper Canada, with Miscellaneous Notices*. Edinburgh 1842

Angus, Margaret. *Kingston General Hospital: A Social and Institutional History*. Montreal 1973

– "James Sampson." *Dictionary of Canadian Biography/Dictionnaire Biographique du Canada*, vol. IX. Toronto 1976

– "Harriet Dobbs (Cartwright)." *Dictionary of Canadian Biography/Dictionnaire Biographique du Canada*, vol. XI. Toronto 1982

Arfwedson, Carl David. *The United States and Canada, in 1832, 1833 and 1834*. London 1834

Armstrong, Frederick H. *Handbook of Upper Canadian Chronology and Territorial Legislation*. London, Ont. 1967

Armstrong, F.H., H.A. Stevenson, and J.D. Wilson, eds. *Aspects of Nineteenth Century Ontario: Essays Presented to James J. Talman.* Toronto 1974

Arthur, Sir George. *The Arthur Papers,* 3 vols. Toronto 1943-1959

Baehre, Rainer. "Origins of the Penitentiary System in Upper Canada." *Ontario History* 69, 3 (1977): 185–207

Baldwin, George R. Report on Supplying the City of Quebec with Pure Water: Made for the City Council by Order of George Okill Stuart, Esq., Mayor of Quebec. Boston 1848

Ball, N.R. "The Technology of Settlement and Land Clearing in Upper Canada Prior to 1840." PhD thesis, University of Toronto, 1980

Barclay of Ury, Captain R. *Agricultural Tour in the United States and Upper Canada.* Edinburgh and London 1842

Barker, Edward John. *Observations on the Rideau Canal.* Kingston 1834

Barrett, Harry B. *The 19th-Century Journals and Paintings of William Pope.* Commentary by J. Fenwick Landsdoune. Toronto 1976

Bathurst Courier and Ottawa General Advertiser. Perth 1841

Beattie, John M. *Attitudes Towards Crime and Punishment in Upper Canada, 1830–1850: A Documentary Study.* Toronto 1977

Bell, Michael. *Painters in a New Land.* Toronto 1973

Bell, Rev. William. *Hints to Emigrants, in a Series of Letters from Upper Canada.* Edinburgh 1824

Bigsby, John Jeremiah. *The Shoe and Canoe; or, Pictures of Travel in the Canadas, Illustrative of Their Scenery and of Colonial Life; With Facts and Opinions on Emigration, State Policy, and Other Points of Public Interest,* 2 vols. London 1850. Republished New York 1969

Bilson, Geoffrey. "Strong Medicine." *Horizon Canada* 9, 11 (1985)

Bingley, William. *Travels in North America, From Modern Writers.* London 1821

Birrell, Andrew. *Canadian Photography, 1839–1920.* Toronto 1979

Blaney, William Newham. *An Excursion Through the United States and Canada During the Years 1822–23.* London 1824

Bonnycastle, Sir Richard H. *The Canadas in 1841,* 2 vols. London 1841. Republished New York 1968

Bouchard, Antoine. "Joseph Casavant." *Dictionary of Canadian Biography/Dictionnaire Biographique du Canada,* vol. X. Toronto 1972

Bouchette, Joseph. *The British Dominions in North America,* 2 vols. London 1832. Republished New York 1968

Bourne, G. *The Picture of Quebec.* Quebec 1829

British American Land Company. *Information Respecting the Eastern Townships of Lower Canada.* Sherbrooke 1836

– *Views of Lower Canada, 1836.* Sherbrooke 1836. Republished 1962

– *Report of the Provisional Committee of the British American Land Co.* London [1832]

– *Report of the Court of Directors to the Proprietors. London 1834*

British Colonist. Toronto 1841

Brydone, J.M. *Narrative of a Voyage With a Party of Emigrants, Sent Out From Sussex by the Petworth Emigration Committee to Montreal, Thence Up River Ottawa and Through the Rideau Canal to Toronto, Upper Canada.* London 1834

Buchan, W.F. *Remarks on Emigration: More Particularly Applicable to the Eastern Townships of Lower Canada,* 2nd ed. Devonport 1832

Buckingham, James Silk. *Canada, Nova Scotia, New Brunswick, and the Other British Provinces of North America.* London 1843

– *Autobiography of J.S. Buckingham,* 2 vols. London 1855

Buckley, Daphne. "Perth: Case Study of a Small Town." BA thesis, Carleton University, 1968

Buckner, Philip. "Charles Edward Poulett Thomson, 1st Baron Sydenham." *Dictionary of Canadian Biography/Dictionnaire Biographique du Canada,* vol. VII. Toronto 1988

Burroughs, Peter. *The Canadian Crisis and British Colonial Policy, 1828–1841.* Toronto 1972

– "Tackling Army Desertion in British North America." *Canadian Historical Review,* 61, 1 (1980): 28–68

Bytown Gazette and Ottawa and Rideau Advertiser. Bytown 1841

Campbell, Frank W. *Canada Post Offices 1755–1895.* Lawrence, Mass.: Quartermain Publications 1972

Canada Company. *A Statement of the Satisfactory Results which Have Attended Emigration to Upper Canada.* London 1841

– *Lands in Upper Canada To Be Disposed of by the Canada Company.* London 1839

Canada in the Years 1832, 1833, and 1834: Contains Important Information and Instructions to Persons Intending to Emigrate Thither in 1835; by an ex-settler. Dublin 1835

Canada Steamship Lines Ltd. *Catalogue of the Manoir Richelieu Collection of Canadiana.* Montreal 1930. Supplement 1931

Caniffe, W. *The Medical Profession in Upper Canada,* 3 vols. Toronto 1894

Careless, J.M.S., ed. *Colonists and Canadians.* Toronto 1971

– *The Pre-Confederation Premiers: Ontario Government Leaders, 1841–1867.* Toronto 1980

Chapman, H.S. *Thoughts on the Money and Exchanges of Lower Canada.* Montreal 1832

– *Recent Occurrence in Canada.* Republished – Montreal 1969

Chasse, Beatrice. "Antoine Légaré." *Dictionary of Canadian Biography/ Dictionnaire Biographique du Canada,* vol. X. Toronto 1972

Chasse, Sonia, Rita Girard-Wallot, Jean-Pierre Wallot. "John Neilson." *Dictionary of Canadian Biography/Dictionnaire Biographique du Canada,* vol. VII. Toronto 1988

Chatham Weekly Journal. Chatham 1841

Chronicle & Gazette. Kingston 1841

The Church. Toronto 1841

Cline, Beverley Fink, ed. *Louisa Clark's Annual, 1841.* Erin, Ont. 1976

Cockburn, Henry. *Memorials of His Time.* Edinburgh 1872

Coke, Edward Thomas. *A Subaltern's Furlough: Descriptive of Scenes in Various Parts of the United States, Upper and Lower Canada, New Brunswick and Nova Scotia, During the Summer and Autumn of 1832.* London 1833

Coleman, John, ed. *Everyday Life in 19th Century Ontario.* Toronto 1978

Coleman, Thelma, and James Anderson. *The Canada Company.* Stratford 1978

Colonial Office. *Correspondence re Affairs of Canada.* London 1840

Counsel for Emigrants, and Interesting Information from Numerous Sources Concerning British America, the United States, and New South Wales, 3rd ed. Aberdeen 1838

Cours D'Histoire ... A l'usage des écoles chrétiennes, 1st ed. Montreal 1841

Craig, G.M. *Upper Canada: The Formative Years, 1784–1841.* Toronto 1963

– "John McCaul." *Dictionary of Canadian Biography/Dictionnaire Biographique du Canada,* vol. XI. Toronto 1982

– "Two Contrasting Upper Canadian Figures: John Rolph and John Strachan." *Proceedings and Transactions of the Royal Society of Canada,* Fourth Series, XII (1974): 237–48

Creighton, Donald. *The Passionate Observer.* Toronto 1980

The Cultivator Magazine. Albany, NY, 1841

Dahl, Edward, Hélène Espesset, Marc Lafrance, et Thiery Ruddell. *La Ville de Québec, 1800–1850.* Ottawa 1975

Daubeny, Charles Giles Bridle. *Journal of a Tour Through the United States, and in Canada, Made during the Years 1836–38.* Oxford 1843

Davis, John. "The Development and the Decline of the Port of Kingston." BA thesis, Carleton University, 1967

Davison, Gideon Miner. *The Fashionable Tour: A Guide to Travellers Visiting the Middle and Northern States, and the Provinces of Canada,* 4th ed. Saratoga Springs 1830

Dawson, Robert Peel. *Extracts from Letters and Journals of Robert Peel Dawson, in England, Canada and U.S.A. 1830–1840.* London 1840

DeRos, John Frederick Fitzgerald. *Personal Narrative of Travels in the United States and Canada in 1826.* London 1827

DeVeaux, Samuel. *The Traveller's Own Book to Saratoga Springs, Niagara Falls, and Canada.* Buffalo 1841

Dickens, Charles. *American Notes for General Circulation.* New York 1842

Domett, A. *The Canadian Journal of Alfred Domett.* Edited by E.A. Horsman and Lilian Rea Benson. Republished London, Ont. 1955

Doyle, M. *Hints on Emigration to Upper Canada; Specially Addressed to the Middle and Lower Classes of Great Britain and Ireland,* 2nd ed. Dublin 1832

Drew, Benjamin. *The Narratives of Fugitive Slaves in Canada.* Toronto 1972

Dufour, Pierre Marc Ouellet. "James McKenzie." *Dictionary of Canadian Biography / Dictionnaire Biographique du Canada,* vol. VIII. Toronto 1985

Durham, John George Lambton. *Report on the Affairs of British America.* Ordered by the House of Commons to be printed, 11 February 1839. London 1839

Erickson, Charlotte. *Invisible Immigrants.* Coral Gables, Florida 1973

Evans, Francis A. *The Emigrant's Directory and Guide to Obtain Lands and Effect a Settlement in the Canadas.* Dublin 1833

The Examiner. Toronto 1841

Fairplay, Francis. *The Canadas as They Now Are: Comprehending a View of Their Climate, Rivers, Lakes, Canals, Government, Laws, Taxes, Towns, Trade, etc.; by a Late Resident.* 1833

Fergusson, Adam. *Practical Notes Made during a Tour in Canada, and a Portion of the United States in MDCCCXXXI.* Edinburgh 1833

Fowler, Marian E. "Susan Mein (Sibbald)." *Dictionary of Canadian Biography/Dictionnaire Biographique du Canada,* vol. IX. Toronto 1976

Fraser, R. "Like Eden in Her Summer Dress: Gentry, Economy and Society, Upper Canada, 1812–1840." PhD thesis, University of Toronto, 1981

Garrison of Quebec, Royal Regiment. *Standing Orders for the Garrison of Quebec.* Quebec 1831

George, V. Alan. "The Rideau Canal 1832–1898." MA thesis, Queen's University, 1972

Gibbs, C.R. Vernon. *Passenger Liners of the Western Ocean.* London 1952

Glazebrook, G.P. de T. *Life in Ontario: A Social History.* Toronto 1968

Godfrey, Charles M. "Elam Stimson." *Dictionary of Canadian Biography/ Dictionnaire Biographique du Canada,* vol. IX. Toronto 1976

– *Medicine for Ontario: A History.* Belleville, Ont. 1979

Godley, John Robert. *Letters from America,* 2 vols. London 1844

Gooderich, Samuel G. *Peter Parley's Travels in Canada; and What He Saw There.* London c. 1850

Gould, Nathaniel. *Emigration,* 2nd ed. London 1834

Great Britain Commissions for Emigration. *Information Published by His Majesty's Commission for Emigration, Respecting the British Colonies in North America.* London 1832

Guillet, Edwin C., ed. *The Valley of the Trent.* Toronto 1957

Gullett, D.W. *A History of Dentistry in Canada.* Toronto 1971

Hanley, Cliff. *History of Scotland.* London 1986

Harris, J.H. *Observations on Upper Canada Collection.* Toronto 1836

Harris, R. Cole. *Two Societies: Life in Mid-Nineteenth Century Quebec.* Toronto 1976

Harris, R. Cole, and John Warkentin. *Canada before Confederation.* New York, London, and Toronto 1974

Harris, Robin S. *A History of Higher Education in Canada 1663–1960.* Toronto 1976

Hawkins, A. *Picture of Quebec: With Historical Recollection.* Quebec 1834

Head, Sir Francis Bond. *The Emigrant.* New York 1847

– *A Narrative by Sir France B. Head,* 2nd ed. London 1839

Henry, Walter. *Trifles from My Port-Folio, or Recollections of Scenes and Small Adventures During 29 Years' Military Service in the Peninsular War ... and Upper and Lower Canada; by a Staff Surgeon,* 2 vols. Quebec 1839

– *Events of a Military Life: Being Recollections After Service in the Peninsula War, Invasion of France, the West Indies, St. Helena, Canada, and Elsewhere.* London 1843

Hodgetts, J.E. *Pioneer Public Service: An Administrative History of the United Canadas, 1841–1867.* Toronto 1956

Hodgins, J. George. *Documentary History of Education in Upper Canada.* Toronto 1897

L'Hôtel-Dieu de Montréal, 1642–1973. Cahiers du Québec, no. 13. 1973

Houston, Susan E. "Politics, Schools, and Social Change in Upper Canada." *Canadian Historical Review* 53, 3 (1972): 249–71

Howard, Richard B. *Upper Canada College 1829–1979: Colborne's Legacy.* Toronto 1979

Hunter, Frank. "The Settlement of the Townships of Charlottenburg and Lancaster in Glengarry County, 1784–1860." BA thesis, Carleton University, 1968

Jackson, John N. *St. Catharines, Ontario: Its Early Years.* Belleville, Ont. 1976

Jameson, Mrs A.B. *Winter Studies and Summer Rambles in Canada,* 3 vols. London 1838

Jefferys, Charles W. *A Catalogue of the Sigmund Samuel Collection of Canadiana and Americana.* Toronto 1948

Johnson, J.K. "The U.C. Club and the Upper Canadian Elite, 1837–1840." *Ontario History* 69, 3 (1977): 151–68

Johnson, Leo A. *History of Guelph 1827–1927.* Guelph 1927

Jones, Elwood, and Douglas McCalla. "Toronto Waterworks, 1840–77: Continuity and Change in Nineteenth-Century Toronto Politics." *Canadian Historical Review* 60, 3 (1979): 300–23

Jones, R.L. *History of Agriculture in Ontario.* Toronto 1946

Journals of the Legislative Assembly. 1841

Judd, William W., ed. *Minister of the London Mechanics' Institute, 1841–1895,* Occasional Papers 23. London 1976

Karr, Clarence. *The Canada Land Company Early Years: An Experiment in Colonization.* Toronto 1974

Katz, Michael B. *The People of Hamilton, Canada West.* Cambridge, Mass.: 1976

Kenny, Stephen. "Cultural Interchange in the Union of the Canadas." PhD thesis, l'Université d'Ottawa, 1978

Knight, D.B. *Choosing Canada's Capital.* Toronto 1977

- "A Capital for Canada," Research Paper no. 182. Chicago, University of Chicago, Department of Geography, 1977

Lacelle, Claudette. "The British Garrison in Quebec City as Described in Newspapers from 1764 to 1840." *History and Archaeology* 23. Ottawa 1979

Lafrance, Marc, and David-Thierry Ruddel. "Physical Expansion and Socio-Cultural Segregation in Quebec City, 1765–1840." In Gilbert A. Stelter and Alan F.J. Artibise, eds., *Shaping the Urban Landscape.* Ottawa 1982

La Minerve. Montreal 1841

Lande, Lawrence Montague. "A Checklist of Early Publications Relating to Public Health and Medicine in Canada in the Private Collection of Lawrence Lande." *Lawrence Lande Foundation for Canadian Historical Research,* no. 5. Montreal 1968

- *The Lawrence Lande Collection of Canadiana ... Montreal 1965*

- *Rare and Unusual Canadiana.* First supplement to the Lande Collection. *Lawrence Lande Foundation for Canadian Historical Research,* no. 6. Montreal 1971

Langton, H.H., ed. *A Gentlewoman in Upper Canada: The Journals of Anne Langton.* Toronto 1950

Laughton, David. "A Historical Geography of Smith Falls." BA thesis, Carleton University, 1970

Leblond, Sylvio. "James Douglas." *Dictionary of Canadian Biography/ Dictionnaire Biographique du Canada,* vol. XI. Toronto 1982

- "La Médicine dans la province de Québec avant 1847." *Les Cahiers des Dix* 35 (1970): 68–95

Lessard, Michel, and Huguette Marquis. *Encyclopédie de la Maison Québécoise.* Montréal 1972

Light, Beth, and Allison Prentice, eds. *Pioneer and Gentlewomen of British North America 1713–1867.* Toronto 1980

Literary and Historical Society of Quebec. Transactions to 1843

- Annual Report etc. of the Literary and Historical Society of Quebec. 1831–63

London Correspondence Inward from Sir George Simpson 1841–2. Introduction by John S. Galbraith. Hudson's Bay Record Collection, 30. London 1973

Lower, Arthur R.M. *Great Britain's Woodyard: British America and the Timber Trade.* Kingston and Montreal 1972

Lower Canada. *Minutes of Evidence Taken under the Direction of the General Commission of Enquiry, for Crown Lands and Migration, Appointed on the 21st June, 1838 ... by Lord Durham ...* Quebec 1839

Lyell, Sir Charles. *Travels in North America, in the Years 1841-2,* 2 vols. New York 1845

McCalla, Douglas. "Isaac Buchanan." *Dictionary of Canadian Biography/ Dictionnaire Biographique du Canada,* vol. XI. Toronto 1982

– *The Upper Canada Trade, 1834–72: A Study of the Buchanans' Business.* Toronto 1979

Macdonald, Norman. *Canada, 1763–1841: Immigration and Settlement.* New York and Toronto 1939

McGregor, John. *British America,* 2 vols. Edinburgh 1833

McIlwraith, Thomas F. "The Logistical Geography of the Great Lakes Grain Trade, 1820–1850." PhD thesis, University of Wisconsin 1974

McKenzie, Ruth. "Laura Ingersoll (Secord)." *Dictionary of Canadian Biography/Dictionnaire Biographique du Canada,* vol. IX. Toronto 1976

Maginnis, Arthur. *The Atlantic Ferry.* London 1892

Martin, Ged. *The Durham Report and British Policy.* Cambridge 1972

Martin, Robert Montgomery. *History, Statistics, and Geography of Upper and Lower Canada.* London 1838

Mattingly, Paul H., and Michael B. Katz, eds. *Education and Social Change: Themes from Ontario's Past.* New York 1975

Mechanics' Institute Board Meetings, 1840–48

Miquelon, Dale, ed. *Society and Conquest: The Debate on the Bourgeoisie and Social Change in French Canada, 1700–1850.* Toronto 1977

Montreal Almanac or Lower Canada Register for 1830. Montreal 1829

Montreal, Common Council. *By-Laws, Rules, Regulations, and Ordinances of the Common Council of the City of Montreal.* Published by order of the Common Council. Montreal 1833

Montreal Gazette. Montreal 1841

Montreal Herald. Montreal 1841

[Montreal] Literary Garland. Monthly. John Lovell, publisher

Montreal Mechanics' Institution. Constitution and Laws of the Montreal Mechanics' Institution. Montreal 1833

Montreal Natural Historical Society. Act of Incorporation and By-laws of the Natural Historical Society of Montreal. Montreal 1833

The Montreal Transcript. Montreal 1841

Moodie, Susanna. *Roughing It in the Bush; or, Life in Canada,* 2 vols. London 1852

The Morning Courier. Montreal 1841

Morris, James. *Pax Britannicus: The Climax of Empire.* London 1968

Morton, W.L. *Shield of Achilles.* Toronto 1968

Murray, Hugh. *An Historical and Descriptive Account of British America.* Edinburgh 1839

– *History of British America, Comprehending Canada, Upper and Lower, N.S., N.B., Newfoundland, P.E.I., the Bermudas, and the Fur Countries,* 3 vols. Edinburgh 1839

Murray, John. *The Emigrant and Traveller's Guide to and through Canada.* London 1835

Murray, Lindley. *The English Reader; or Pieces in Prose and Verse; Selected from the Best Writers.* Montreal 1840

– *A First Book for Children.* Quebec 1838

Nader, George A. *Cities of Canada, vol. I: Theoretical Historical and Planning Perspectives.* Toronto 1975

Neatby, Hilda. *Queen's University: 1841–1917: And Not To Yield,* ed. Frederick W. Gibson and Roger Graham. Montreal 1978

Need, Thomas. *Six Years in the Bush; or Extracts from the Journal of a Settler in Upper Canada, 1832, 1838.* London 1838

Newell, Dianne. "William Gooderham." *Dictionary of Canadian Biography/Dictionnaire Biographique du Canada,* vol. XI. Toronto 1982

The Niagara Chronicle. Niagara 1841

Niagara Reporter. Niagara 1841

Nish, Elizabeth. *Debates of the Legislative Assembly of United Canada, 1841–1867,* vol. I. Montreal 1841

The North American Tourist. New York 1839

O'Brien, Mary Sophia Gapper. *The Journal of Mary O'Brien, 1828–1838,* ed. Audrey S. Miller. Toronto 1968

O'Leary, Rev. Peter Michael. *Guide to the Quebec Model Made by Jean-Baptiste Duberge, R.E., and restored by Lt. Col. Reverend P.M. O'Leary.* Quebec 1918

Ouellet, Fernand. *Economic and Social History of Quebec, 1760–1850.* Toronto 1980

– *Lower Canada, 1791–1840: Social Change and Nationalism.* Trans. Patricia Claxton. Toronto 1979

Passenger Act, 9 Geo. IV. c. 21. This act was repealed during the session of 1835 by an act then passed, the 5 and 6 Will. IV., c. 53

Pavie, T. *Souvenirs atlantiques: Voyage aux Etats-Unie et au Canada,* 2 vols. Paris 1833

Picken Andrew. *The Canadas, as They at Present Commend Themselves to the Enterprising Emigrants, Colonists, and Capitalists.* London 1836

Pickering, Joseph. *Inquiries of an Emigrant.* London 1832

Porter, John R. "Joseph Légaré." *Dictionary of Canadian Biography/Dictionnaire Biographique du Canada,* vol. VIII. Toronto 1985

Prentice, Alison. *The School Promoters: Education and Social Class in Mid-Nineteenth Century Upper Canada.* Toronto 1977

Present State of the Canadas: Containing Practical and Statistical Information re the Climate, Soil, Produce, Agriculture, Trade, Currency, Banking, etc., of Upper and Lower Canada, Useful for the Emigrant, Merchant, and Tourist. London 1833

Prospectus of Lands in Upper Canada to be Disposed of by the Canada Company. 1841

Québec. Les Archives du Québec: Inventaire général des Archives du Québec. Don de M. Bernard Weilbrenner en 1971

Quebec Gazette. Quebec 1841

Quebec Mercury. Quebec 1841

Radcliff, T., ed. *Authentic Letters from Upper Canada.* Dublin 1833. Reprinted Toronto 1953

Raudzens, George. *The British Ordinance Department and Canada's Canals, 1815–1855.* Waterloo 1979

Reamon, G. Elmore. *A History of Agriculture in Ontario,* 2 vols. Toronto 1970

Report of Quebec and St Andrews Railroad Association. 1837

Report of the Immigrant Committee of Montreal, L.C., for 1840. Montreal 1840

Report of the Select Committee of the Legislative Council of Upper Canada. Toronto 1835

Review of Facts and Observations Made by Naturalists, Botanists, Historians, and Travellers, on the Properties and Production of the Sugar Maple Tree. London 1832

Richardson, John. *Eight Years in Canada: Embracing a Review of the Administrations of Lord Durham and Lord Sydenham, Sir Chas. Bagot, and Lord Metcalfe.* Montreal 1847.

Report of the Special Sanitary Committee of Montreal upon Cholera and Emigration for the Year 1834. Montreal 1835

Report on the Canal Navigation of the Canadas. By Lieutenant-Colonel Phillpotts, Royal Engineers. Printed in the fifth volume of papers on subjects connected with the duties of the Corps of Royal Engineers. [London] 1842

Robertson, J. Ross. *What Art has Done for Canada.* A guide to the J. Ross Robertson Collection in the Toronto Public Reference Library, 2 vols. Toronto 1917

Robinson, J.B. *Canada and the Canada Bill, Being an Examination of the Proposed Measure for the Future Government of Canada, with an Introductory Chapter Containing some General Views re the British Provinces in North America.* London 1840

Rolph, Thomas. *A Descriptive and Statistical Account of Canada: Showing Its Great Adaptation for British Emigration.* London 1841

Ross, Eric. *Beyond the River and the Bay.* Toronto 1970

Sabine, E. *Report on the Meterology of Toronto.* 1845

St. Catharines Journal, and Welland (Niagara District,) General Advertiser. St Catharines 1841

Samuel, Sigmund. *The Seven Years War in Canada, 1756–1763.* Toronto 1934

Saunders, Robert E. "John Beverley Robinson." *Dictionary of Canadian Biography/Dictionnaire Biographique du Canada,* vol. IX. Toronto 1976

Schull, Joseph. *Rebellion: The Rising of French Canada 1837.* Toronto 1971

Scott, C. Thoughts on the Government, Union, Danger, Wants and Wishes of the Canadas; and on the Proper Line of Policy of the British Parliament in these Respects: Being a Letter to Mr. Hitchings of Toronto, etc. Montreal 1839

Scrope, G. Poulett. *Memoirs of the Life of the Rt. Hon. Lord Sydenham.* London 1843

Senior, Elinor. "The British Garrison in Montreal in the 1840s." *Journal of the Society for Army Historical Research* 52, 210 (1974): 111–27

– *British Regulars in Montreal: An Imperial Garrison, 1832–1854.* Montreal c.1981

– "The Influence of the British Garrison on the Development of the Montreal Police, 1832 to 1853." *Military Affairs* 43, 2 (1979): 63–8

Sequel to the Counsel for Emigrants. Aberdeen 1834

Shepperson, W.S. *British Emigration to North America.* Oxford 1957

Shirreff, Patrick. *A Tour through North America.* Edinburgh 1835

Simpson, Sir George. *Narrative of a Journey Round the World, During the Years 1841 and 1842,* 2 vols. 1847

The Sixth Annual Report of the Board of Directors of the Grand River Navigation Company. May 1841. St Catharines 1841

Sketch of the Caledonia Springs, Upper Canada, printed for the proprietors by J. Starke and Co. Montreal 1839

Smith, Mary Larratt. *Mr. Smith in Upper Canada.* Toronto 1980

Smyth, Coke. *Sketches in the Canadas.* London 1842

Snow, Thomas Hailes. *Reflections on the Moral and Civil Condition ... North America.* Niagara 1841

Spendlove, Francis St George. *The Face of Early Canada.* Toronto 1958

Splane, Richard B. *Social Welfare in Ontario, 1791–1893.* Toronto 1965

Statement of the Satisfactory Results which Have Attended Emigration to Upper Canada, from the Establishment of the Canadian Co. until the Present Period, 3rd ed. 1842

Stevenson, Hugh A. "Thomas Thompson." *Dictionary of Canadian Biography/Dictionnaire du Canada,* vol. IX. Toronto 1976

Stewart, Charles H. *The Eastern Townships ... Bibliography.* Montreal 1940

Stewart, J. Douglas, and Ian E. Wilson. *Heritage Kingston.* Kingston 1973

Strickland, S.M. *Twenty-Seven Years in Canada West, or the Experiences of an Early Settler.* London 1854

Stuart, James. *Three Years in North America,* 2 vols. Edinburgh 1833

Talbot, Edwin Allen. *Five Years' Residence in the Canadas,* 2 vols. London 1824

Taylor, C.J. "The Kingston, Ontario Penitentiary and Moral Architecture." *Histoire Sociale/Social History* 12, 24 (1979): 385–408

Taylor, C. James. "Poisoned Pen." *Horizon Canada 8, 86.* Quebec 1985

Taylor, Henry. *Considerations on the Past, Present and Future Condition of the Canadas,* no. II. Montreal 1839

Templeton, Frederick. *Statement Made to a Special Court of the Directors of the British American Land Company, Held on the 3rd of February 1836.* 1836

Thompson, John. "The First Last Spike." *Horizon Canada* 4, 43. Quebec 1985

Thompson, Zadock. *Geography and History of Lower Canada.* Stanstead and Sherbrooke 1835

Thomson, William. *A Tradesman's Travels in the United States and Canada, in the Years 1840, 41, and 42.* Edinburgh 1842

Tocqueville, Alexis de. *Democracy in America,* 2 vols., ed. Phillips Bradley. New York 1945

– *Journey to America. Trans. George Lawrence and ed. J.P. Mayer.* London 1959

Tocqueville au Bas Canada, presentée par Jacques Vallée. Montréal 1973

Toronto. *The City of Toronto Poll Book, Exhibiting a Classified List of Voters at the Late Great Contest for Responsible Government.* Toronto 1841

Toronto. *Committee for Relief of the Poor and Destitute of the City of Toronto,* 1st and 2nd Reports. Toronto 1837

Toronto Curling and Skating Club. *The Canadian Curler's Manual; or, An Account of Curling as Practiced in Canada, with Remarks on the History of the Game by James Bicket.* Toronto 1840

Toronto Female Benevolent Society. *The Annual Report of the Toronto Female Benevolent Society.* Toronto 1840

Toronto Foresters' Society. *Rules and Regulations of the Foresters' Society for the Relief of the Sick Brethren.* Toronto 1839

Toronto General Hospital. *Rules and Regulations Proposed for the Governing of the General Hospital.* York 1830

Toronto, Ordinances, etc. *Ordinances of the City of Toronto, 1834.* Wm. L. Mackenzie, mayor. Toronto 1834

Toronto Patriot. Toronto 1841

Traill, Mrs C.P. Backwoods of Canada. Being Letters from the Wife of an Emigrant Officer, Illustrative of the Domestic Economy of British America. London 1839

Trofimenkoff, Susan Mann. *The Dream of a Nation: A Social and Intellectual History of Quebec.* Toronto 1982

Tulchinsky, Gerald. "George Moffatt." *Dictionary of Canadian Biography/Dictionnaire Biographique du Canada,* vol. IX. Toronto 1976

- *The River Barons: Montreal Businessmen and the Growth of Industry and Transportation 1837–53.* Toronto 1977
- ed. *To Preserve and Defend: Essays on Kingston in the Nineteenth Century.* Montreal and London 1976

Turner, John F. "River Landscape Changes in Building the Rideau Canal at Long Island and Hogs Back." BA thesis, Carleton University, 1970

Turner, Wesley B. *Life in Upper Canada.* Toronto 1980

Upper Canada Gazette. Toronto 1841

Upper Canada Herald. Kingston 1841

Vansittart, Jane, ed. *Lifelines: The Stacey Letters, 1836–1858.* Don Mills 1976

Vigne, Godfrey T. *Six Months in America.* London 1832

Wait, Benjamin. *The Wait Letters.* Introduction by Michael Cross. Erin, Ont. 1976

Watson, Aldren A. *The Village Blacksmith.* New York 1968

Wells, W.B. *Canadiana: Containing Sketches of Upper Canada and the Crisis in its Political Affairs.* London 1837

The Western Herald. Sandwich 1841

Willis, Nathaniel P. *Canadian Scenery Illustrated, from Drawings by W.H. Bartlett, the Literary Department by N.P. Willis,* 2 vols. London 1842

Wilson, J. Donald, Robert M. Stamp, and Louis-Philippe Audet. *Canadian Education: A History.* Scarborough 1970

Wood, J. David, ed. *Perspectives on Landscape and Settlement in Nineteenth Century Ontario.* Toronto 1975

Woodcroft, Bennet. *A Sketch of the Origin and Progress of Steam Navigation.* London 1848

Index